The God Hater

discovering life after death

Rebecca Dinsmore
with Allison Althauser

The God Hater: *Discovering Life After Death*
by Rebecca Dinsmore & Allison Althauser

www.thegodhaterbook.com

All rights reserved
Copyright © 2012 by Rebecca Dinsmore
Cover Artwork © 2012 by Scott Althauser

Book Design & Layout © 2012 by Scott & Allison Althauser

No part of this book may be reproduced or transmitted in any form or by any means, electronic or mechanical, including photocopying, recording, or by any informations storage and retrieval system, without the written permission of the publisher, except where permitted by law.

ISBN 978-0-9850628-0-4
ISBN 978-0-9850628-1-1 (ebook)

*To my family,
friends, and spiritual community
who gave me permission to be real.*

I do not fear either pain or death.
What do you fear, lady?
A cage.

> ~ *Eowyn of Rohan*
> *(J.R.R. Tolkien)*

Contents

- 9 — Backwords and Forewords
- 23 — Between the Lines
- 37 — The Betrayal
- 47 — Honorable Mention
- 63 — Trap Doors
- 73 — A Widow's Reproach
- 83 — Grief Group Happy Hour
- 95 — Red Birds & Grey Goose
- 105 — The Great Purge
- 111 — Daily Quiet Times
- 119 — Cabo Wabo Christmas
- 129 — The Veil
- 137 — F*** the Neighbors
- 145 — 12 Doughnuts & A Switchblade
- 153 — Peace Treaty
- 165 — The Waiting Game
- After Life

Chapter 1

Backwords & Forewords

[When the time comes] God will not look you over for medals, degrees, or diplomas, but for scars.

~ Elbert Hubbard

Another day in paradise had ended. The late night revelers were tucked away in bed, sleeping off the exotic resort festivities, while I walked along the grainy sands of a now vacated beach.

Pacing myself with the free flow of liquor, I had drunk my fair share, successfully maintaining a healthy buzz throughout the evening, but not enough to knock me out like countless times before. If I wanted my plan to work, I had to keep what wits I had left on reserve for this very event. Then at last, when the vengeful deed was done, my mind and soul could find some peace.

An empty horizon of blackened sky and sea stretched into eternity, patiently waiting for my arrival, hungrily eyeing my defeated soul with every intention of swallowing me whole. Even if I wanted help, I had ventured too far away from the outdoor lounge area for anyone to see me or hear a despairing cry. I was not trying to escape the inevitable. I didn't care anymore.

A welcoming wave of the cool, dark sea washed over my sandy bare feet, offering illusive tidings of eternal comfort and rest, urging me forward as it retreated and disappeared.

My eyes followed the restless shoreline that led to the infamous stone arch. The half moon hung low and eerily still, embellishing the rocks' enormity with deceptive silhouettes. I knew the depths of the surrounding water were sufficient for serving its purpose, as I moved toward the final destination in front of me; all I had to do was shut down the natural survival instinct to swim to the surface.

...Just sink and wait for my breath to run out.

My heart pounded painfully in my chest, as if knowing it too would soon be silenced forever, desperately pleading in vain for the life it had left to live, but only reminding me of a life I couldn't live and was ready to end.

Glancing a few yards behind me, I had to be certain the pair of sandals and room key remained where I placed them. I had intentionally set my identifying items just beyond the reaching tides. The sandals were still sitting there, but I couldn't see if the key had stayed put as the shifty shades of night made it difficult to distinguish between shells, debris, and my belongings.

I squinted back again, angry at the thought of having to distance myself from my objective. Part of the plan was letting them know those were my things and that, without a doubt, I was gone.

"Damn it!" I cursed irritably at myself. "Where is the key, I've lost the frickin' key!"

I dug aggressively through each section of my over-sized purse that served more like a carry-on travel bag than an accessory. "Where the hell is it?!"

I felt like Mary Poppins peering deep inside my pseudo suitcase as if there was some unseen storage space to the thing. I wished I could just stamp my foot once or twice and the key would magically appear.

It was nearly noon on the first Friday of the New Year at the Family Community Center, people coming and going at their leisure. I was too frantic; add a pinch of stubbornness and a dash of pride, to ask any of the passerby's for help. The renovated outreach center, formerly known as the county hospital, housed a few of Simply Grace's training rooms where we regularly taught group classes and semi-annual conferences. Just across the street sat the main headquarters and counseling offices of Simply Grace, Inc., our non-profit organization I had co-founded.

After attending my first conference eight years ago, I had fallen in love with this ministry. I went through the basic class and continued on to the advanced training (both were nine-month courses) and had earned the certification to be a counselor and teacher.

Now I did volunteer-work alongside a great team. Our days were booked with people who, in one way or another, wanted help; something more or different for their lives, or sometimes just needed a human being who would listen. I was helping teach the morning class that had started four months before and we had our first retreat that weekend.

With all the presentation supplies ready and waiting by the van, I reached in my pocket for the key that I knowingly stuck in there minutes before, but it was gone.

I cannot believe this is happening right now. Here I am, leading a women's retreat, and I can't even keep track of the stupid key!

I continued the silent monologue, checking every pocket of my jacket and pants. Climbing into the van again, I scanned the cup-holders, under the front, middle and back seats, and then ran my fingertips inside the soft folds of the blue velour cushions. No key, just some spare change and a gooey candy wrapper. I felt the panicky feeling in my gut growing after each failed search attempt.

Trying to settle down and refocus, I shut my eyes momentarily and felt the sunshine warming my face. It was a pleasant 60 degrees on the first weekend of January. This was what we Georgians call the January Thaw, and, whether we had any real winter weather or not, it was our mini-spring-break.

The holiday stress and insanity was behind us, thank God, and all the festive décor was packed away in the attic to sit for another year. I felt good knowing the rather daunting task of Christmas tear-down would not be waiting for me when I came home; especially after this kind of trip.

Standing there alone in the middle of the parking lot, too upset to cry, I considered the possibility that I may have just done it for real. In a matter of five seconds, I had lost the one and only key to our precious Blue Bell.

I stared blankly at the ancient conversion van, trying to ignore the irritating helplessness gnawing at my she-woman complex. Out of all the people that used this thing, I was not going to be the one that ended Her era of servitude.

My first impulse was to whip out my cell phone and call Ben, my go-to man for anything. He always knew what to do. The same time and energy I spent running around in a hot mess, reacting with whichever emotion the issue provoked, my husband would spend assessing the situation and jumping right into fix-it mode. We were yin and yang when it came to problem solving. While I would worry about what to do, he would already be doing it.

However, Ben was at work right then and a good forty-five minutes away in Friday afternoon traffic. So for the first time in a long time, or maybe the first time ever in our marriage, I decided not to call Ben.

I can handle this, I thought as I let go of the phone in my pocket and my hotline to commonsense. I was back to square one. Pacing dejectedly around the van, and feeling a swift kick to my headstrong ego, I threw my hands up in forfeit and contempt.

"Okay Jesus," I huffed impatiently, "this is your retreat. I'm doing this for you. These are your ladies and I'm not calling Ben. I'm depending on you, you've gotta help me."

What did I think he could actually do for me that instant? I wasn't at church working the prayer lines during altar calls, commanding deliverance and divine healing, or slaying some unsuspecting, newbie member in the Spirit.

I was alone at a Community Center, angry at my carelessness and, as a last-ditch effort, asking God for a personal favor. And, I figured if I phrased my request by putting the people first, then my odds were increased that he would respond.

I am doing this for him after all, isn't he supposed to repay my sacrificial servitude with something good, like my own spiritual vending machine or personalized version of sowing and reaping?

"Move your foot," he said, disrupting my impromptu dogmatic soapbox moment.

I automatically looked down at my feet and saw only a few dry leaves scattered around where I stood. *Did I hear him right; just 'move my foot?'*

With the end of my shoe, I gently nudged one of the leaves aside. Stunned by what the leaf revealed, I bent down and squinted in disbelief and amazement at the glorious key. *He did it; he really answered me.* I shook my head in awe and pure relief, chuckling out loud with embarrassment at my private hissy fit. The dark cloud of frustration and fear lifted from my head and the tight knot in my stomach melted away. I was okay, I didn't have to involve Ben, and the retreat was still on.

I crossed the street into the counseling office driveway and parked near the back entrance. Cutting off the engine, I made sure every door was unlocked and, leaving no way of escape this time, left the runaway key in the ignition.

Once inside, I turned on a couple lights and waited while my eyes slowly adjusted from the bright sun. I had the entire floor to myself. After working longer days Monday through Thursday, we always had an extended weekend off, with the exception of class retreats. Normally we scheduled the first retreat mid-October to jump-start bonding time and breeze by the making-acquaintance-phase in their relationships.

However, DeeAnn, my co-leader and partner in crime, had been in the middle of building a house for Habitat for Humanity and worked every weekend through the holidays. She had asked if we could postpone the retreat until after the New Year's. This was a big ask, especially when the thought of the busy season kicked my blood pressure up a few notches, but I agreed.

We were heading to Joan and Doug's, my sister and brother-in-law, house that was nestled in the valley of a beautiful mountain range in North Georgia. Since no one was interested in proving their survival skills by camping and roughing it with Mother Nature, the mountain house was a happy medium for all.

I went into my office to review our lecture notes for group times and quietly sat down at my desk. As I drew in a deep breath, I felt the inviting stillness settling around me. The peace that resided in this room was simply intoxicating. With each inhale, the zoetic silence filtered through, numbing any sense of time or agenda while gently ushering me into the present tense. I relished these moments and quickly learned to seek them out, as my thoughts miraculously collected themselves and my whole being becomes centered, focused, in-sync.

With my Bible and a fresh blank page of legal pad in front of me, I was trying to wrap my head around and write down what God had told me to teach for our concluding devotion on Sunday. I quickly began scribbling away.

When I felt everything was complete and in order, I knew there was just enough time to call Ben before the ladies arrived. Back at the front desk, I picked up the landline phone and dialed his work number.

"Hey Bek."

"Hey, how're you?" I smiled, adoring how casually he answered, knowing I would be on the other end.

"I'm good," he responded with a worn voice. "Ready to head home."

Ben was a supervisor at the post office, which started his day at the ungodly hour of 3:00 am, so by this time he was eager to get home, grab something to eat, and crash with a long afternoon nap.

"Well, I'm ready too and just waiting for everybody to get here. What are you going to do while I'm gone?"

"Ride. It's going to be perfect riding weather." He answered as the tiredness in his voice broke with excitement.

Ben's passion was motorcycles and he loved all things Harley Davidson. We enjoyed doing everything together and I had tried getting into the whole biker scene, but it never jived with me. However, I would ride with him once in a while.

I loved that he had a passion. As long as I had known him, since the day we first met in the rural public high school thirty-five years ago, he had been a tried and true rider at heart.

The youngest of five other siblings, I had been raised in an ultra conservative and traditional southern family, topped with my pastor dad and June Cleaver mom. I lived in a petri-dish home. Naturally, this combination had been the ideal breeding ground for my post-pubescent revolt.

Then one day, a mutual friend introduced Ben and me. It was love at first sight. Instantly qualifying as an opposites-attract relationship, we both knew we were made for each other.

He was a long haired, wild hippie who wore bell-bottoms and platform shoes. He was a junior and he rode a motorcycle. I was the classic, naïve sophomore, who had recently ditched the school band and sports teams after discovering that participating in extra-curricular activities was notoriously uncool and lethal to my reputation. He still remembered what I had looked like the first time he noticed me. I had straight, waist-length brown hair that was always parted down the middle, and wore a daringly short, yellow mini-skirt showcasing my long legs.

Four years later, I couldn't get out of the house fast enough and Ben and I had decided to get married. We moved into our own home and were two peas in a pod, madly in love with each other.

As with any couple, we had stressful times and arguments; but even our fighting was passionate, along with the make-up sessions afterward, and our love life in general. Which had eventually led to our first major surprise two years into our marriage; we were pregnant. About eight months later, our first son Josh had arrived, and then several years after him came our second son, Dusty.

Ben adored his sons and I was amazed at how easily he took to the fathering role. He always made sure our parenting responsibilities were shared equally, and was insistent in giving me some precious alone time away from the house.

Josh and Dusty favored Ben and I respectively in both looks and personalities, except for their height. Ben and I stood eye to eye, but the boys had quickly surpassed us during their growth spurts.

They were both very athletic and had excelled in sports. We were those parents that saw every game and had supported anything they wanted to try.

As kids tend to do, our sons grew up; filling out their adolescent frames into strong and sturdy men. Josh had married his wife Karen, and Dusty ventured out west, living and working in Colorado.

Ben and I had survived parenthood, loving that it was just the two of us again, and had already made plans to build a log cabin on the property we owned along the Appalachian foothills. We wanted to live quietly, doing whatever the mood inspired during the week, and then come back to visit our families on the weekends.

We prepared by selling our first and only home of twenty-four years, and moved into our son and daughter-in-law's unfinished basement. In a mere three months, Ben remodeled our new apartment to absolute perfection. I had chosen a modernized farmhouse motif and decorated with denim blue upholstery and furniture, rusty red and khaki curtains and fabrics, with hints of olive green and earth-toned accents. While Ben painted each cabinet set and room with light, neutral colors, complimenting our butcher-block countertops, hardwood floors, and plush area rugs. We had wanted to create a welcoming and relaxed atmosphere and, for now, we thoroughly enjoyed having a smaller, cozier home together.

Even though he had kissed my good-bye this morning before he headed off to work, and I would see him again in two short days, just hearing Ben's voice over the phone made me miss him already.

"Will you miss me?" He asked, reading my thoughtful silence.

"Sure I will."

"Nah!" He replied playfully, "You're going to be so busy with those women, you won't have time to miss me."

"Nooooo. You're going to be having so much fun out riding, you won't think twice about me," I teased back. We both laughed and then fell quiet, knowing we wouldn't talk until Sunday and it was time for us to go.

"I will miss you and I love you," he said with tender affection.

"I'll miss you too Ben. Love you."

We skipped the goodbyes and ended with our usual "see you later". One by one, the women arrived, gathering together in a nervous-excited bunch of energy in the parking lot. I went out to greet them and exchanged hugs and smiles.

"Okay, let's throw whatever you can in the back here," I instructed with directive hand signals, "and then we'll pack the food on top of everything."

Within minutes, the van was packed to capacity, bursting with passengers and luggage. Each seat was occupied and even the aisles were crowded with extraneous who-knows-what. I wasn't comfortable operating such a large, top-heavy vehicle, especially through the mountains, and as luck would have it, one of the women was a retired bus driver and wanted to drive.

Blue Bell was on her best behavior, as if she understood what precious cargo she was carrying, while we twisted and turned our way up the mountain. Fortunately none of us had car sickness as we weaved between the North Carolina and Georgia state lines admiring the beautiful mountain scenery just outside our windows.

We parked under the mountain house davenport and unfolded out of the van. I took a minute to stretch my body and wake my stiff legs. Barely making it past the entranceway, my eyes followed three, huge, grey storage bins full of food along the hallway floor and then landed on DeeAnn.

"Hey y'all! She beamed excitedly, "You made it!"

"What'd you do, bring your whole house with you?!" I teased as we greeted each other with hugs. Whenever food and entertaining were involved, DeeAnn's inner Martha Stewart would come alive. She loved packing to the max with her special utensils, appliances and ingredients.

"Nope, just my kitchen," she grinned, happily turning back to stir her bubbling soups on the stove. As the ladies unpacked the van, I grabbed my bags and tossed them in the upstairs Master bedroom before handing out their sleeping arrangements in the basement.

"Supper's ready in five," I hollered down the stairs, "and feel free to change into some comfier clothes."

A few minutes later, the kitchen suddenly seemed too small with eight women circling the perimeter, ravenously eyeing the food. After devouring dinner and finishing dish duty, the ladies claimed seats on the family room floor, couch, or recliners. I smiled at the picturesque room that looked like a slumber party more than a spiritual retreat. Each woman was dressed in pajamas, cupping warm mugs of coffee or hot chocolate, and cuddled into fluffy pillows and cozy blankets. We turned on the gas-burning fire for extra effect.

I promptly started the first lesson by summarizing everything we had worked on during our classes, which had focused on telling their life stories honestly. After a couple hours of examining the hurts and rejections from their pasts, and finding the resulting lies instilled from those wounds, it was almost midnight.

"You've done so well tonight, but I'm ready for bed. We can wrap this up in the morning. Y'all okay with that?" I asked.

"Yes," they responded, smiling at me with sleepy eyes.

"Alright, you know where everything is, but let me know if you need anything else. Good night."

"'Night," said each one as they filed down to their beds.

Chapter 2

Between the Lines

The spiritual life does not remove us from the world but leads us deeper into it.
~ Henri Nouwen

The next morning, I awoke with Saturday's schedule scrolling through my head, but I was still so tired. I threw on another comfortable ensemble, loafed out to the kitchen, and saw a fresh brewed pot of coffee and a cute display of assorted creamers, sugar, and sweeteners.

Our goal for this specific retreat had been to really pamper and spoil the women. We had worked through serious issues with each one and wanted to make them feel extra-special during their time away from home. DeeAnn said if I taught, then she would plan and prepare the meals and extra goodies. I couldn't handle being Betty Crocker and Mother Teresa all weekend, so that agreement was fine by me.

After a refreshing breakfast spread of yogurt, freshly cut fruit, cereal, and bagels, we finished the Identity Lesson from the night before. I was thankful to see how God was working in all of us, and that each woman was open and receptive for personal revelation and healing.

We ate a quick lunch and decided to stretch our legs and venture out for a mid-afternoon stroll. When we returned, DeeAnn had set up at-home pedicure stations with foot baths, loofahs, foot scrubs, and nail polish. After our pedicures, red wine and cheesecake tarts were served to each woman, signifying our modified version of the traditional washing of feet and partaking of communion ceremonies. Another few hours of focused interaction had passed and we were already ending the discussion on real forgiveness.

"Until the wounds are recognized from our pasts, we live out of those hurts today. We learn to cope and are never free to be our true selves. This is why forgiveness has an essential role in discovering who we really are," I said in conclusion. "Forgiveness is embracing our pain and being honest with those who hurt us, even ourselves, even God, and letting everything and everyone off the hook."

The women listened intently as they were realizing they all had someone to forgive. I went on to explain that most people, including myself, had less difficulty forgiving others, and struggled the most with forgiving themselves and God.

Everybody was snuggled up in their designated spots, pencils and pens at rest on their notebooks, while they sat in a reverential hush of deep contemplation; I knew it was time to be done for the day. Our Saturday night movie was Tyler Perry's, "Diary of a Mad Black Woman". Not only did it provide some comical relief, but the story also relayed a powerful message of forgiveness that complimented the evening lecture. By the end of the movie, I was fighting to keep my heavy eyelids lifted. As soon as everyone said their good nights and parted ways, I collapsed into bed and instantly fell asleep.

When Sunday morning arrived, I was excited that we were almost done with the retreat, and eager to get home and see Ben. Throwing on my last casual outfit of the weekend, I pulled back my short, unruly hair into a semi-pony-tail and walked out to find the ladies ready to start the day.

After a hodge-podge breakfast of leftovers, we gathered back in the family room. Angling the cheap wooden easel and gigantic white note pad just right for everyone to see, I randomly selected the first culprit to begin the exercise.

"Why me?! I wasn't raising my hand?" She argued with a smile.

"Why, what are you scared of? After all we've been through...?"

"Ugh! Fine. Somebody pass me the tissues," she teased back dramatically, "I was really hoping all the crying was over since it's our last day."

"You'll be okay, it won't hurt too much, I promise." I winked, and then wrote her name in big fat black letters, centering it on the blank sheet of paper. Then I explained since the majority of the weekend had been spent discovering who they were not, now it was time to confirm (and affirm) their true identities in Christ. I wrote down every word around her name as each woman, including the teachers, spoke truth about their classmate.

"Thanks you guys," she said, gently dabbing the corners of her eyes. "Y'all don't know how much this means to me." She looked over at me with mascara trails running down her cheeks and pointed towards her paper, "Can I keep that?" She sniffled.

"Of course you can!"

She stood up and tore off her sheet. "I should've known not to waste time putting on my make-up this morning. I'm a mess!" Laughter immediately erupted and, after that, the women were eager for their turns.

When we finished the group time, the ladies wanted to dance and started pushing back the couch, chairs, and end tables. Forming two rows of four on the improvised dance floor, we cranked up the music and fell in sync to the electric slide.

An hour of sporadic dancing and bursts of contagious laughter had flown by when I remembered we still had to clean up and squeeze in the closing devotion. I volunteered to handle the kitchen area while the other ladies divvied out the remaining chores. Once the dishes were washed and dried, I saw the phone sitting under the cupboards.

Should I call Ben? I wondered, glancing at the clock and at the thermometer hanging outside by the kitchen window. *11:40 am, sunny, 59 degrees. Nope. He is definitely out riding.*

I figured if I did call him, he would have to pull off the side of the road, find his cell phone, try to hear me and talk over the street noise; not an ideal conversation. I would see him in a few hours anyway and he knew where I was and that I was safe. Dismissing the thought, I finished wiping down the counters, folded the dirty rag over the sink divider, and gathered the ladies in the family room for our final meeting.

With the notes I had prepared Friday afternoon in front of me, I opened with the passage from 2 Corinthians, chapter 4. I likened the passage to a miner who struck gold or discovered diamonds. The miner would clean, polish and take great care in the newfound treasures. As wives, we had to cherish the treasure in our husbands, just as they are and not how we think they need to be. My challenge to them was speaking love to their spouses through support, honor and most importantly, respect. In doing so, the diamond in the rough could appear.

I subtly checked the time on my watch: *12:20 pm, two hours behind schedule.* DeeAnn quickly blessed us out in a closing prayer, and everyone left to load their luggage into the van. I looked around the house to make sure no one had left any personal belongings anywhere, and when I came back into the living room, the ladies were dragging their heels and just standing around talking. Apparently they didn't want the weekend to end.

"Look," I said in all seriousness as their chatter stopped abruptly. "Y'all can stand here and gab all day, but I'm going home to have sex with my husband. So get your asses in the van."

Grinning mischievously, I nonchalantly walked straight through the stunned group. Embarrassed chuckles broke the awkward silence as they followed suit and piled inside Blue Bell. My volunteer driver hopped in the captain's chair and turned the key in the ignition, but the engine didn't crank. She turned it again. Still nothing. She tried a few more times with no response.

"Blue Bell!" I snapped, as if scolding her would make her start up. "Come on. You have got to be kidding me!" Somehow the battery was dead, even though I had checked several times over for any lights left on.

"Everybody sit tight. I'll take care of this," I sighed frustratingly. I knew I was more eager to get home than they were, so I kept my anger at the troublesome vehicle to myself and avoided eye contact with them. There was only one person I could think of to give us a jump, our faithful watchman and gatekeeper to the resort: the Sky Valley Deputy. In less than ten minutes, our hero of the day had arrived and proficiently began connecting the jumper cables. With one turn of the key, the old van roared back to life. We left the engine idling and surrounded the Deputy, thanking him incessantly for his services. He smiled bashfully, clearly over-whelmed by so much estrogen and attention, tipped his tan brimmed hat, and wished us a safe trip home.

Leaning back against the headrest, I watched quaint little towns and wide landscapes of country foothills stretch by my window. I felt myself unwinding as my "spiritual leader and mother" state-of-mind transitioned back into normal, everyday life. I was spent on every level, but the experiences of revelation and growth during the weekend had redeemed all the effort of preparation and follow through.

As gratitude and thankfulness quickly refilled my emptiness from the retreat, I marveled at how God had been revealing himself throughout the class, and the resulting transformations taking place in them now. While the ladies reflective discussions consumed the ride back, my thoughts drifted to my husband. The readiness, borderline impatience, to see Ben and be in my own home and bed tonight was building. I felt the excitement heightening as we neared our destination.

Without a hitch, we were in the Simply Grace parking lot unloading our belongings. When the last lingering embrace had been given, the women headed their separate ways, and I was alone at last. I quickly went inside, unpacked the leftover food in our kitchenette, put away the easel and drawing pad, and locked up the office. All I had left to do was drop off Blue Bell, pick up my Jeep, and I was finally home free.

I turned in to my niece's driveway at 4:30 pm Sunday afternoon, nearly two and a half hours later than I had told Ben I would be home, but I was too happy to care.

Parked in the grass next to the first turn-around, was my early fiftieth birthday present: a shiny bright red Jeep. Ben couldn't wait for another year and decided to buy me a brand new Wrangler right after I had turned forty-nine years old. The Jeep had been washed, waxed, and was now sparkling in the late afternoon sunshine.

What a man, I thought, admiring his small surprise for my return.

I spotted my niece crouched down in her garden by the garage, but instead of coming out to greet me, she remained focused on the hardened dirt. I backed into the second turn-around, parking the big van as best as I could, and waited for Kristy to at least acknowledge I was here; but she kept digging at the barren ground.

Why is she poking around the garden in the first week of January anyway? I wondered.

As I reached over to shut off the van, Kassie, my other niece, was silently standing in front of my window. Startled by her sudden appearance, I noticed that her face was worn and puffy with dried tears staining her blotchy cheeks.

"What's wrong?" I asked her with concern, while rolling down the window.

"Get out of the van," she said softly but sternly.

By-passing her demand, I asked a second time, "*What's* wrong?"

"*Bek*, get out of the van," she repeated in an eerily controlled tone while motioning her hands forward at me.

Ignoring her again, I wanted to know what had happened. The first person coming to mind was my mother because she was aging and her health had been declining.

"Mom?" I guessed.

"No. *Get out of the van.*"

I didn't understand why she insisted on waiting until I was standing next to her before she could deliver the news. Finally obliging to her request, I turned off the engine and stepped out onto the pavement.

"Is it Josh?" I asked with more urgency.

"No," she answered delicately, looking off into the distance with an uncomfortable stare.

I felt a strange, fearful panic intensifying with each of her negative responses. "Dusty?"

Her lips began quivering as fresh tears filled her eyes and streamed down her face. She briefly glanced at me and confirmed it wasn't about Dusty. The painful anxiousness broke from my gut and was now coursing through my veins.

If it isn't mom or my sons, then there's only one person left. My heart raced at the thought and I was too scared to voice his name, but I had to know, she wasn't telling me otherwise.

"Ben?" I finally asked, feeling my eyes and body shudder in preparation for her response.

"Ben?!" I screamed again, afraid to look ahead of me, "No!"

"Yes!"

"Do not go out there. No. Let me off right this instant!" I insisted nervously, staring out at the uninterrupted flat terrain.

I knew this was a lake and, even if there had been months of sub-zero temperatures with several feet of snow cover, I had no intention of testing its sustainability. Or worse yet, discovering the lake's hidden weak spot and plunging into the freezing waters below.

"Yes we are. We'll be okay!" He shouted through his helmet, while revving the snowmobile's engine. I could only see his hazel eyes flashing with excitement over his facemask. "It's gonna be fun. I won't let you get hurt," he laughed, winking back at me, "Don't worry!"

Before I could object again, he pressed the throttle all the way down and we took off with a jump. I automatically wrapped my arms tightly around his stout waist, squeezing my eyes shut in terror as we ripped through layers of the blinding white powder. I peeked behind me to see if the rest of the family had followed in our wake of snow dusted cyclones, and they were already beside us, ready to pass by and trail-blaze around the pristine frozen tundra. We had just visited the highest point of our tour through the mountain backcountry, capturing an awesome family picture with the snow-capped, stunning mountain range sitting behind us.

Three days earlier, we had arrived in Park City, Utah. The city was abuzz because the annual Sundance Film Festival, quite possibly the most thrilling event that happened out here, had ended a few days ago. Everywhere we visited, the star struck locals dutifully reminded us that we had just missed the action and could've seen all the famous people from Hollywood.

We had spent the first two days skiing and snowboarding around several large resort areas. Katie, Josh and Karen's daughter and our only granddaughter, had never skied before, so that first day I had volunteered to stay back while she took the ski school crash course.

When she completed the class, Ben came back and walked Katie over to the intermediate hill. I watched as he attentively hovered over his granddaughter while she smoothly made her way down like an old pro. After a couple runs, she had wanted to tackle the more advanced slopes, and off she went. An eight-year-old, on her first time skiing, had effortlessly tackled every slope by the end of the day. We were all very proud of her.

In the evenings, we ate local fare at neighboring restaurants, toured the town, and visited Robert Redford's clothing and furniture stores. We wanted to eat at his restaurant as well, but apparently it had caught fire during the film festival. By the third day, our group had tired of skiing and was ready for a change of pace, and so we decided to try out snowmobiling. Ben and I shared one snowmobile, Josh, Karen and Katie took turns with two, and Dusty and his girlfriend had their own.

Even though I was mad at Ben for charging off onto the lake, openly rebelling the way he does, I couldn't help but love his keen sense of adventure. He always made sure I was safe and secure at all times, and in turn, I felt protected whenever I was with him. He was a wild man, fearless and confident, and he somehow managed to do everything with ease, so smooth, steady, and under control no matter what he was up to.

My head remained tucked and burrowed between Ben's shoulder blades as we zoomed over the lake a while longer. When the joy ride had ended and we regrouped on solid ground, I loosened my death grip around my husband's body, and exhaled a sigh of relief; thankful we were all accounted for and in one piece. The guys were smiling, cheeks flushing with windburn and pure exhilaration. As I looked at the men in my life, cherishing Josh and Dusty and their carefree spirit that naturally came from Ben, I paused to let this moment stand still.

With the fantastical scenery surrounding us, and the glistening layers of snow enhanced by the added touch of brilliant sunshine, I felt incredibly blessed to have a family that not only got along, but also had a blast together, truly enjoyed one another's company, and loved each other. Our son and daughter-in-law were happily married and adored their daughter Katie. Our second son was thriving with his new life and passions out West. And Ben and I were celebrating a restful and intimate season together.

Of course, we all had difficult times, life hadn't been easy breezy, but we struggled our way through the tough spots. However, I was grateful and thankful for the valleys because in the end, we had survived and grew closer as a family unit. Who could ask for more?

The tour guide waited patiently for us to catch our breath and asked if we were ready to keep going, and seven helmets nodded back at him in agreement. We gradually tooled our way down the gorgeous Uinta Mountain, snaking through long stretches of winding trails, and finally made it back to the rental office. After checking in the sleds, we grabbed our personal items from the lockers nearby and hitched a ride on the public transportation back to our lodge. The family agreed to quickly shower and change so we could go out to eat because, by this time, we were famished after a long day spent outdoors.

For our last night and dinner together, we picked a local barbecue joint and when everyone had their fill, instead of site seeing in the city, we headed back to the lodge and start packing. We had an early flight to catch in the morning and, in true Dinsmore fashion, our clothes and winter gear were strewn everywhere and would require the rest of the night to pack.

With our suitcases and travel bags ready by the door, I turned off the lights and crawled under the pile of blankets, snuggling my freezing toes in between Ben's warm legs and feet. We cuddled in the bed for a few minutes, while my toes thawed, and reminisced about the amazing family trip that seemingly flew right by.

"I'm glad you had a good time," he said quietly.

"Me too," I whispered back, as we smiled and held each other in the dark.

We instinctively exchanged our good night kisses, knowing we were both too tired for any late night relations. Ben fell sound asleep within seconds, as evidenced by his soft snoring, while I slowly unwound from the excitement of day and eventually drifted off to sleep.

The next morning, we met up with the family at the lobby, luggage in tow, and busted our butts to the shuttle. We had booked an early flight to avoid getting stuck in the crazy afternoon Atlanta traffic. An hour later, we were dropped off at the airport and checked in at our airline's front desk. We weaved through the security checkpoint and started our mad dash to the designated terminal.

I must have unknowingly been power walking down the long hallway because when I looked over to see if my family was keeping pace, I didn't recognize any of the faces next to me.

"Wait up!" I heard Ben holler from somewhere behind me. "Get back here with us!"

Chapter 3

The Betrayal

One should rather die than be betrayed. There is no deceit in death. It delivers precisely what it has promised. Betrayal, though...betrayal is the willful slaughter of hope.
         ~ *Steven Dietz*

"Bek, come on. Come back to us!" He yelled again, but I didn't want to come back.

I felt miles away, floating on the shores of nothingness, but a voice was echoing out to me. My mind was fighting hard to remain in the comfort of this emptiness, but I did not know why.

"She's coming back!" He cried as blood rushed life back to my face, painting over the ashen shades of white. "She's coming back!"

Coming back from what? I wondered, still clinging to the darkness by keeping my eyes closed.

"Come on Bek," he pleaded again. I knew that voice; but it wasn't Ben's.

I forced my eyes open as they gradually focused on my nephew's figure leaning over me. I felt his hands cradling my head and his eyes were filled with some sort of devastated expectancy. *Why does he look so awful?*

I felt the grass and cool earth beneath me and recognized the hand-laid sidewalk stones next to my arm. This was our sidewalk, to our home.

Why is Jason holding me on the ground? How did I get here? I couldn't even remember the drive back to our house.

I propped up on my elbows with my eyes darting around wildly. People were everywhere, standing around the front yard, but maintaining a safe distance.

What?! Why are all these people here and why does everybody look so terrible? I could still feel Jason's eyes on me too.

"Jason, stop looking at me. What are you looking at me for?" I demanded in frustrated bewilderment.

"Nothing. Nothing." He said quickly, averting his stare from my disoriented state. "You with me?"

What does he mean?

"Jason, I'm with you," I assured him, but he wasn't backing off. I started to wonder what more he wanted from me.

"Are you with me?" He persisted again.

My god. Where the hell else would I be? I thought, becoming slightly irritated.

"Yes. I'm wi…" I started, but then the scenes began flashing in front of me like a slide show.

I had been at Kristy's house, parking Blue Bell, but Kassie was the one that greeted me. She was ill and wouldn't tell me what was wrong. I had to pull it out of her. As the memory manifested, I felt a disabling blackness creeping over my consciousness. We went through the list of family members and I had left off asking about Ben.

"Yes," she managed to whisper.

"Is he hurt?"

Willing herself to respond, she had shaken her head no, and then she started sobbing. I knew there was more she couldn't tell me.

If something was wrong with Ben and he wasn't hurt, what else was there?

Without thinking, the next question had flown out of my mouth, "He died?!" I cried at her hysterically.

I watched her head carefully nod yes and remembered I looked up at the sky, unable to grasp the horror of what that nod had meant. My brain had tried forming words, but my voice would not cooperate. From somewhere deep within me, an agonized scream had erupted into the air, stealing any remaining ability to function as it left my lungs. I had collapsed in a lifeless form and didn't felt the impact of my body hitting the ground. The panicked cries above me had faded away, and I drifted off into a vapid state of unconsciousness.

He wasn't hurt. She said he died. *Ben's gone! He's dead!*

I felt the truth of those words snapping me back to present tense and my head swam in disbelief. *How could this be? This cannot be! No. Not this time.*

I fiercely rejected the reality of what was happening and suddenly everything became crystal clear. *Of course! It's not true. Ben is fine. They are lying to me.* I slowly turned my head back to Jason, who was still sitting next to me on the ground, and leveled him with my stare.

"Nope. *You're* wrong. Wrong guy." I said in clever defiance, "The cops have made a mistake. Ben will be here in a minute, you watch." I stood up in all my dignity and pride, brushing off a few spots of dirt, and marched over to the front side of the wrap-around porch.

"I'm sitting here until he comes home," I declared, perching myself on the bottom step, "you watch. You just watch."

While I sat on the steps waiting for Ben's arrival, swarms of people appeared, their cars were lining the streets on both sides. There were so many faces, so many people I didn't even recognize.

Where were they coming from? Why were they here?

I tried ignoring the onlooker's and their sideways glances, observing every move I made, but a subtle anger was building inside me as their hushed tones and worried conversations scratched at my ears. A pastor showed up carrying a Bible and, immediately zeroing in on him, I silently dared him to step one foot closer. Fortunately Jason caught him in time, quickly steering the pastor away before he could approach me, and sent him home. They had no reason being there. Nothing was wrong and we were fine.

Frustrated, I got up from my look out and went around to the groups of people, informing them that they needed to leave because my husband would be home soon and I had to cook dinner for him. As I made the rounds, I noticed my son and daughter-in-law walking in from the street. They had to park down the road because their own driveway was blocked with so many cars. I ran up to Josh and grabbed onto his arms in desperation. I knew my son would tell me the truth. I had to know.

"I know you'll shoot it to me straight Josh. Tell me!" I pleaded, "Tell me it's not true!"

Holding me at arm's length, he looked into my eyes with a sad but wary stare, like he was trying to protect his mother from unavoidable pain.

"Momma…he's gone," he said solemnly, shaking my shoulders lightly as if it would help the truth settle in, but I wasn't listening. I didn't want to hear.

"He's gone," he repeated softly to me.

"No," I cried back at him. No. I would not accept it. They had the wrong Dinsmore. *Yes, that's it. People are always messing up the spelling of our last name.* "No. It's *D-e*! They've got it wrong. It has to be a Densmore, not Dinsmore. It's not him!" I argued, wailing madly as my limbs went limp again, but Josh caught me before I hit the ground.

"No mom, it's dad," he said pulling me to my feet, holding me up and looking at me urgently, "I just saw him. I saw the body. He's dead."

The unbearable grief and defeat took control of my being and I could not move or think. All I felt were heaving sobs of torment wracking my body as someone carried me inside our home and away from the gawking crowd. I was gingerly sat down on the living room couch as I wept uncontrollably.

The next few hours were a trippy mess of shock and denial. One minute I realized Ben was dead and would instantly fall to pieces, and a second later I would confidently maintain that he would be coming home any time now.

I was also frantic to see my other son, frequently asking for Dusty's whereabouts, and when I was reassured each time that he had caught the first flight home, the answer never registered. Someone even reminded me that Dusty and I had just spoken on the phone before he boarded the plane in Colorado, but I didn't remember talking to him.

The blur of people funneling in and out only intensified the continuing nightmare, observing me curiously like some circus sideshow. At times, I would return their provoking stares, unable to discern their faces. I could physically see and hear the activity around me, but everything felt so surreal. I could not get up and leave or close my eyes at the scary parts. With no way of escape, I was forced to sit and watch as this horrible reality unfolded.

I heard my other sister, Faye, guarding the door that led down to our basement, repeatedly turning good-intenders and well-doers away, but somehow someone had let my mom come in to see me and I cringed at the sight of her. As she scooted within inches of my face, I prepared myself for her draining demeanor and tactless comments.

"You're gonna get through this," she croaked, "I got through it and you're gonna get through it…"

I blinked at my mother, willing her to just shut up, but she continued, "You can't go around this. You can't back up. You have to go through it."

When she was done, I wished they would get her out of my house. I was having enough trouble trying to accept that I wasn't seeing my husband tonight. I wasn't ready to hear how I would get through any of this when the thought of living another minute made me want to die.

Soon after, my cousin sat down beside me; he was one person I was waiting for and actually wanted to see. He looked at me softly, knowingly, gently wrapping his arm around my shoulder while we sat in a long breath of precious silence.

"God is about to show you things in the spirit world that you never would've imagined," he said in quiet confidence, "You won't believe how you'll see angels and things that you don't even know exist, because once somebody that you love has crossed over, then God lets you see."

I accepted his consoling words and felt strangely connected to him because he understood, he had been there. A few years ago, his twelve-year-old son had died suddenly when his heart exploded walking down the hallway. Like any other day, he had kissed his son good-bye and left for work. A couple hours later, his son was dead. No warning. No good-bye. No nothing. And then it hit me.

Ben must have left me a good-bye. Maybe a letter, a card, a trinket or something. He had to have known he wouldn't see me again. He always made sure I knew exactly where he was in case his plans changed or if there had been an emergency. He wouldn't have left me without saying good-bye; that wasn't like him.

I charged over to my bedroom door in an anxious frenzy. One or two family members jumped up to follow me, trying to divert my determined hysterics so I wouldn't look like an insane person. But I *was* crazy and could care less who was watching as I began ripping our room apart. I tore through both of our wooden dresser drawers, nightstands, closets, bathroom cupboards, and under the bed, desperately searching for some semblance of a farewell.

The one's who tried to stop me must have given up because I heard my brother close the door to give me privacy. "Let her be." He told them defensively, "She needs this."

He stood watch in the thresh hold until everything in my room was demolished. I came out empty handed and slumped onto the couch in exhausted defeat.

Dusty arrived around 1:00 am, and I felt momentary relief that finally, both of my sons were safe and we were all together under one roof. When I first saw him, the apparent devastation in his eyes broke me into heavy sobs again as we embraced, holding each other, rocking and crying. There were no words.

As I watched him sink to the floor, weeping by my feet, I wondered what his long plane ride back had felt like, knowing what he had to come home to, and the life he would later leave behind.

Another couple hours passed and everybody was ready to take a break from grieving. Joan had called my doctor for a prescription to drug me up so I could sleep, but I refused to take them.

I had watched mom check out, trying to escape her grief with pills after dad died from cancer. Twenty years later, she still had not fully recovered. Her method of coping only fueled my resolve. I wanted to remember what this first night felt like. I wasn't going to numb out or miss the pain and I made sure God knew what he was up against.

"You got me into this!" I threatened viciously, "And you're gonna fucking get me out."

No one was leaving me alone tonight in case I tried sneaking off to kill myself, so Reba, my good friend of twenty-five years, stayed in the room as I changed into some pajamas and crawled into bed. I couldn't recall seeing her before now; but I wasn't surprised she was here.

Reba was a spitfire woman whom I lovingly termed the most dangerous species known to man: a redneck with money. She also had a fierce, overly protective at times, maternal instinct. She would just as soon miss her own wedding than not be with me tonight.

She settled into one of the over-sized chairs, occasionally filling the disheartening silence with lighter, mindless chitchat, while I lay comatose under the covers. Then my bedroom door opened and my nieces, Karen, and Joan filed in dressed in their pajamas.

"Move over," Kassie ordered playfully, pointing me towards the middle of the bed.

"Why? No. What are y'all doing in here?"

"You're not sleeping alone tonight. We're staying with you," she replied matter-of-factly while they sandwiched me on the bed.

I tried persuading them to sleep anywhere else in the house besides my room, but they were insistent. Holding onto my sister Joan's hands, I did not let go the entire time as we laid there, five women deep, huddled together across my bed.

I listened to the soft breathing of human life surrounding me as I pushed my nose into the pillow, taking a deep inhale of Ben's sweet, woodsy scent. I had dug through the dirties, pulled out one of his faded red t-shirts, and carefully slid it over my pillow so I could feel close to him. After thirty-one years of sleeping with my husband, this was it, there were no more nights together. The realization that Ben would never again be next to me in our bed was too much to comprehend.

Lying wide-awake in the pitch black, I felt an invisible force pressing into my chest, smothering what will I had left to stay alive from my body. I was too weak to resist the looming weight, helpless against its frightening power.

I couldn't live like this. I did not want to survive. I could end this pain tonight. I knew there was a way out and I would be with Ben forever. Death was all I could feel and it looked better than any life existing in me now. The desire to kill myself felt oddly comforting and quickly consumed my thoughts. As a plan began taking form, I felt a gentle squeeze on my hands, disrupting the macabre, transfixing spell that had fallen over me.

I opened my eyes and saw Joan looking at me tenderly, as though she knew where my mind had wandered. Silent tears fell from both our eyes while we laid in bed, crying together until dawn.

Chapter 4

Honorable Mention

A word will never be able to understand the voice that utters it.

~ Thomas Merton

Late Monday morning, most of the family had left while I remained in bed, dazedly staring at the dormant ceiling fan for hours. We had an appointment at the funeral home to make arrangements, but I couldn't motivate myself to move. Suddenly, out of nowhere, Reba barged in again, walked straight into my bathroom and turned on the shower. Without a word, she came right over to me, picked me up out of bed, stripped off my clothes, and threw me into the shower.

"You got ten minutes and then I'm comin' back to get you out," she commanded, yanking the shower curtain closed behind me.

I was too stunned to respond as the hot water poured over my naked body. Closing my eyes, I felt the steady water massaging my neck and shoulders as the images and information about Ben's accident swirled around in my head. My sons had sat me down earlier to explain Ben's accident, but the details sent me reeling into another mind-meld of shock. I did not know how much more my brain could absorb.

According to the official report, Ben had been on his motorcycle crossing a nearby overpass that had two adjoining intersections on either ends. When the first light turned green, he obviously left the intersection, heading towards the next light. The car that hit him had taken the wrong exit. Instead of performing a legal U-turn another block down the road, the driver had continued on, planning to cross four lanes of traffic when Ben was approaching from his left. The driver willingly ran the red light and was arrested for second-degree vehicular homicide at the scene.

The investigators reported that Ben had been driving 10 mph when he was hit. I tried to understand how he had died from the impact if he was riding that slowly. Ben always wore his helmet and was a very careful and aware rider. He must have been hit just right and that was all it took.

Georgia Bureau of Investigations took his body to a morgue for the official autopsy in order to verify the cleanliness of his body. They ran toxicology reports to rule out any drugs or alcohol that might have been in his system, then his vital stats for any indications of a heart attack or stroke.

I could not stand the thought of these strangers poking and probing my husband's body when I had not even seen him yet, but the thought of actually seeing his empty form made me sick to my stomach. I dreaded that moment because then his death would be true; but I also felt tortured having to wait. We had no idea how long the autopsy would take or when they would release his body because of the extensive testing, but we had to proceed with the viewing and funeral planning anyway.

I managed to finish showering and dress myself, after convincing Reba I could handle that much, and we arrived at the prominent funeral home right on time. The funeral home director was friends with Josh and knew our family. When we walked inside, he was standing in the spacious foyer ready to greet us.

After expressing his condolences and gently assuring us he would take good care of the family, the director led my sons and me back where the coffins were stored. When he turned on the overhead lights, an intimidating display of open caskets met our eyes. Every size, style and finish, every fabric and color of interior, even tiny models for babies and children. I began panicking as I looked around this ominous room crammed with body boxes.

I felt my knees buckling and quickly steadied myself on a nearby table. The director noticed my reaction and pulled out one of the wooden chairs for me to sit down and catch my breath. For once, I couldn't settle down and take charge. I never imagined that shopping for my husband's coffin would be an item to cross off from my to-do list. I couldn't even remember how to spell family member's names for the obituary, much less pick out a complimenting fabric color for Ben's corpse, so I let my sons handle the task.

I watched as Josh and Dusty carefully walked around the room, pausing at one coffin, talking over it, then moving on to another, delicately and thoughtfully deciding which option was best-suited for their dad. I knew in some way these decisions were part of their grieving process.

"Hey mom," Josh called quietly from across the room, "I promise we won't have a blanket of flowers with those cheap plastic phones that say 'Jesus called and Ben answered'." He smirked, knowing how much I hated those tacky things.

Instead, I chose a blanket of long stem red roses in memory of the thirty red roses Ben sent me for our thirtieth anniversary last September. We discussed the schedule for the viewing and funeral service. The one thing I was adamant about was having only one night of viewing. I didn't want to drag anything out, but the director politely disagreed. "We had to bring in a volunteer just to check the voicemails and return calls," he said respectfully. "There are three hundred messages asking about Ben's funeral arrangements and that's only from the past four hours. We won't be able to handle the crowds we're anticipating, even with extra help."

While he continued explaining that we would have to conduct two nights of viewing, I stared at him completely dismayed, trying to figure out how these masses of people had known Ben. I told the director I understood and consented to the new schedule, but I was fuming inside.

> Was one viewing night too much to ask? Why did the crowds get to dictate our arrangements? Shouldn't the wife and family have priority?

We finished the meeting after discussing a few other minor details and on the ride home, I felt the exhaustion down to my bones. Once I was back in the long-awaited privacy of our basement apartment, I walked straight into my bedroom and groaned loudly, flinging myself across the inviting bed. I was drained, irritated and just wanted to sit in my room and block out the world; however, Josh had told me there were family and friends my sister and brother-in-law's house waiting to see me tonight. The last thing in the world I wanted to do was be around more people.

Haven't I been through enough for one day? I thought, angrily rolling my eyes. *I don't give a shit about these people. They can wait until next year to see me for all I care, or better yet, how about never?!*

An hour later, I was led back into the car. During the drive over to my sister's house, Josh said that Ben's mom and dad, Granny and Pop, had been asking to see me, but everybody decided they should wait until tonight. Ben's family had to remove and hide all the guns from Pop's house because he was threatening to kill himself. When Pop found out his son had died, he broke and became suicidal. The family was concerned that his unstableness could affect my own fragility, but I didn't care what Pop had threatened because I was thinking the same things.

Walking between rows of cars parked in Joan and Doug's long driveway and yard, I paused by the sunroom door just outside of their depressingly cheery yellow house. As I tried convincing myself I would be okay, I saw the white picket fence Ben had built for her front garden, a small group of smokers gathered by the garage, and the sun setting below the tree line, reminding me that I had lived through the day and this evening would soon be over.

Subtly entering through the kitchen, I found a seat on the sofa and was determined to stay there until we could go home. I tried to be present as people approached and fed me all sorts of redundant sympathies, but grief kept me distant and safely detached. I mindlessly watched people mingle and snack on the deli food Joan had ordered when I noticed a fidgety, plump little man positioning himself in the closest corner possible to me.

Discreetly turning my head in the opposite direction to avoid another shallow encounter, I saw my father-in-law heading towards the sofa. As he gingerly sat down beside me, it became obvious this unfamiliar guest in the corner was not going to budge. While Pop and I were talking, consoling each other, the preacher just stood there in his priggish, pastoral posture, staring at us.

Pop finally noticed the intruder's awkward presence and told me he had invited his friend to come along for support. Then he leaned in closer to me and croaked, "That's our preacher Bekki."

I disdainfully glanced back at the man, disguised in a black suit and white-collar, clutching his Bible like he was interviewing for the job. I felt the anger igniting inside me. I was mad at this stranger: mad at what he represented, mad at the vacant corner he weaseled in to, and mad at the way he observed us through his darkened, beady eyes.

"Do you want him to do the service?"

With as much respect as I could muster for my husband's dad, I steadily replied, "No. I don't. I've already handled that Pop. Jason's doing the service."

There was absolutely no way in hell that was going to happen. Pop submissively retracted his offer while preacher-friend remained at his post the entire night, keeping his brow slightly furrowed with plagiarized concern.

Rescuing me from further unsolicited, empty conversations, Josh and Karen drove me back home. No sooner did we step foot through my front door, when I asked Karen, "You got vodka?"

"Yah. I do." My responsible daughter-in-law answered.

"*Good*," I said willfully, "get ready to start mixing."

I needed something to take the edge off, I hadn't eaten or slept in over thirty-six hours, and I was ready to be done. Realizing that trying to stay sober through the next few days was for the birds, I eagerly discarded my resolve from the previous night. I was not a drinker by any stretch, maybe the occasional glass of wine or margarita if we were out to eat, but tonight I was thirsty. A few screwdrivers later, I was calming down and felt much better. I even laughed once or twice.

After her guests had left, Joan had come over to stay with me through the night, armed with sleeping and anti-anxiety pills and, not putting up a fight this time, I washed the prescriptions down with another screwdriver. I laid in the darkness not totally awake or asleep, just floating in a weird state of semi-consciousness watching the hours crawl by and wishing I didn't have to face another day.

Tuesday morning dawned and Joan was already awake and busy making coffee to ease my hangover. I dared not move from the warm safety of my pillow and blankets. I had no desire to do anything but stay in bed; however, it wasn't long until Joan noticed I was still lying there and forced me out.

I went into the bathroom to brush my teeth and to make myself look somewhat presentable. Pulling open our bathroom drawer, I saw my toothbrush sitting there by itself. Warm tears brimmed my eyes as my strength to stay standing gave way. Bracing myself on the laminate countertop with both hands and tears splashing into the sink, I began remembering the rampage from yesterday afternoon. After I had returned from making Ben's funeral arrangements, DeeAnn was in my house.

DeeAnn was also a strong southern woman and it was a rare occasion that she cried for anything, but when I asked why she was there, her tough exterior cracked wide open, admitting she had folded Ben's laundry and put his clothes away. She had wanted to spare me from another meltdown at the sight of his underwear, and then her anger flared.

"Why?! Why did he do this to you?" She yelled, roughly wiping the tears off of her flushed cheeks, "Why'd he take Ben? Why him?!"

I cried with her as she had repeated the same questions that ticker-taped through my head every other second, in between the suicidal ones. Right then I had realized I would never launder or fold Ben's clothes, or clean or care for any of his things ever again. And I snapped. Storming furiously into the bathroom, I had snatched up anything of his I laid eyes on. Deodorant, baby powder, cologne, razor, toothbrush, contact solution, soap, shampoo. I grabbed all of his toiletries, carried the armloads outside, and angrily threw everything into the trashcan.

Blinking the tears away, desperately trying to regain composure, I started brushing my teeth and gazed in the mirror at the empty reflection staring back. I looked like death. My naturally darker complexion had paled. The usual brightness that lit my brown eyes was now lifeless and dull.

I quickly swept some rosy blush over my inherited high cheekbones, smudged on a few dabs of concealer to hide the grayish under-eye circles, and saved the finishing touches for later. While the hot rollers set in my hair, I reluctantly undressed, exchanging the coveted comfort of my pajamas for obnoxiously confining, black slacks, and a formal blouse.

Surrounded by my little entourage, following me straightaway like a pack of baby ducks, we loaded into the car again and drove back to the funeral home for the private family viewing.

Before I even entered the room, an enlarged portrait of Ben was sitting on display by the doorway. Unnerved by the sight of his life-size face smiling back at me, I stopped to let the swelling emotional wave pass. With my sons and Karen on either side of me, we walked in and nothing could have prepared me for this moment. My eyes were drawn to the opposite end of the viewing room, instantly focusing at the head of Ben's open casket. Sickening fear clenched my stomach as we approached him together. When I saw his face, screams began pouring out of me uncontrollably.

"This is real!" I sobbed, closing my eyes in horror. "This is real, this is real!" I cried over and over again, trying to convince myself I was not dreaming. Dusty immediately crumpled to the ground weeping beside the casket and his Uncle Doug rushed in to pick him up off the floor.

He looked like my Ben. No disfiguration. No bumps, bruises, or scratches. It was Ben and he was dead. He didn't even look like he was sleeping because he had always slept on his side or stomach. And now he was laid on his back.

The rest of both sides of our family gathered around us and we all mourned together, holding each other over Ben's casket, and wept in agony. The weight of our grieving was suffocating me and I wanted to get away and catch my breath. We had a few hours until the public viewing so we decided to escape for a while and get something to eat. Caravanning over to a nearby restaurant, the fifteen of us were seated around a long wooden table.

The server made the rounds, taking down everybody's order, and when it was my turn, I ordered a Texas-style Margarita. Food was the last thing on my mind. I hadn't eaten anything since lunch two days ago. When the meals arrived and the super-sized, pink slushy margarita was set in front of me, I grabbed for it saying, "Yes-ssssss."

"Mom..., uh-uh," Josh said just as I was about to inhale my drink.

I glared across the table at him, "What?!" I asked incredulously.

"No. Don't. We have to meet a lot of people. I need you on your feet," he said patiently with subtle hints of paternal undertone.

"Josh, I am your mother. I want this margarita." I placated sarcastically. Then the whole table piped in trying to take away my drink. I was so tired of everybody constantly telling me what to do, and worse yet, what not to do. It was like I had fourteen mothers smothering me at all times.

"Yes!" I yelled angrily, clutching onto the glass, "I'm drinking the fucking margarita!"

I felt Dusty lay his hand on my shoulder as he came in beside me. "We'll go and buy you one later," he said calmly in my ear as my grip loosened and he gently slid the drink away.

I sat at the table, feeling like a child and silently cussed up a storm while everybody finished their meals.

Why should anyone get to tell me what to do? What gives them the right? I am burying my husband in two days and should be able to do whatever the hell I want.

As we pulled back into the funeral home parking lot, I was amazed at what I saw. Wrapping down the steps, onto the sidewalk and around the building, stood a line of people. Policemen had to block off the main road, directing traffic as people poured in from everywhere. The funeral home provided plenty of parking, but the lot was already over-flowing. Soon the visitors were forced to park and walk from a mile or more away.

We carefully approached the main entrance and Josh and Dusty stood beside me, ushering me in through the front double doors. When we stepped inside, all I could see was navy blue. Standing in the foyer were two lines of a dozen uniformed firemen, forming a tunnel between the crowds and saluting us as we walked through. Apparently they were the honor guard that normally only attended a fellow fireman's funeral, not a parent of a fireman. Never before had I seen or felt anything like this in my life. I was both incredibly honored and humbled.

As we headed towards our designated spots, I asked the funeral director if there were any other viewings tonight, because I could not comprehend how many people were still flooding in. He told me it was just Ben. *This was all for Ben.* I heard my family gasping in disbelief at his response. Instead of having a typical single ceremonial room, the funeral home had opened the partitions, creating a doublewide room. Additional seating had been arranged around the sofas and wingback chairs lined each wall to accommodate the visitors.

A chair was placed by Ben's casket for me, and bossy-pants Reba kept insisting that I needed to sit and rest. However, my rebellion had kicked in and, when I pictured the silent widows seated by their late spouse's casket, I was determined to do the opposite. I stayed standing, met and greeted every visitor through the entire night. I made sure to meet each of the firemen, shake their hand and tell them how much they honored Ben, our family and me. The boys also brought anyone involved with Simply Grace through the line so they could see me.

While the people slowly filed by us, many of them were Ben's friends and co-workers from the post office. I found myself comforting them as they grieved in front of me. I didn't even know most of these people, but they were devastated. One woman told me that every post office that had record of Ben serving or handling audits for them were flying their flags at half-staff. The entire county post office Ben had worked for was shut down while other helpers were hired to get the mailing scheduled and processed. Counselors had been called in as well to help the grief-stricken staff and employees.

They shared with me about how Ben had helped them in some way. Someone didn't have money to refill their propane gas tank one winter and Ben called in the local company and paid the bill.

Another had just moved from Ohio as a single mom with no one to watch her child. Ben had re-scheduled her shift and worked the extra hours for the mother just so she could have a baby-sitter.

I listened in awe and was completely dismayed as one person after another shared their stories. I had no idea he had done any of these things. He never tooted his own horn or called attention to himself. He didn't need to. I thought I was doing these great and mighty things for God, by working with the hurt and needy, but Ben was the one doing what mattered. He was being himself, sharing his natural gifts and talents without expectation, reward, or even acknowledgement.

Hoping we had made some headway after another hour had passed, I looked over the sea of faces and the room was more crowded than before. Reba and Karen made sure I took breaks and escorted me to the bathroom frequently. As we squeezed through the masses, I felt people touching me and trying to talk to me, but Reba and Karen assured everybody I was okay and kept moving me through the rooms.

Somehow my father-in-law's relentless preacher-friend snuck in behind us and I overheard him asking Karen if we had any unsaved members in the family. I was insulted at the audacity of this man who was standing in front of my dead husband, trying to evangelize in the midst of our grief. Before Karen could answer him, I cut in and coolly said, "Yah, right over there," pointing at Doug.

"He's unsaved and an atheist," I added just for spite.

We watched and snickered quietly as he bee-lined over to Doug, cornered him for several minutes, trying to minister to Doug's rootless, dying soul. Either Doug had told him the truth, or the preacher figured out we were screwing with him.

By that time, our true colors began to show. My family's coping tendency in difficult situations was using sarcastic, sick-humor (and liquor, of course, for the less conservative half) to help us in the pain. Any reprieve after two days of the melancholic seriousness was more than welcome. I hated the sympathetic stares in my direction, like I was some wounded, lost puppy. I also hated the feeling of being on display, and the paste-on smiles that never matched the look in everyone's eyes.

Noticing my increasing discomfort, Karen said under her breath, quoting a line from the movie Madagascar, "Just smile and wave boys. Just smile and wave." She stood by me most of the night, providing moments of brighter entertainment and never left my side, except when she started to fidget, and then I would make her go outside for a smoke break.

When the evening was finally ending, Reba volunteered to drive me home and kept another light conversation, mainly with herself, flowing most of the way. She had asked me to think of some ideas or special words for the funeral service. I told her I would while I stared out the window into the darkness.

"Honor." God said, interrupting my thoughts.

What?! I retorted sharply, feeling the anger spike just at the sound of him.

"Honor," he said again.

After all the tears, all the questions I had thrown at him the past two days, he had been silent. I didn't know where he went or what he so busy doing that he couldn't answer me, but now was the first time he decided to say something.

Okay you son of a bitch. You did this, I scowled, *Now what do you want?*

"Before you honor Ben, I want you to honor Matt," he replied patiently.

Matt was our nephew on Ben's side of the family who had recently come home from his third tour in Afghanistan. Including him in the service would never have crossed my mind, but I wasn't about to let God know that.

Fine. I'll do what you tell me to, I said tolerantly, consenting only to his request, *but I'm doing it for Matt, not you.*

Chapter 5

Trap Doors

We almost never hear words that stir life within us, that pour hope into those empty spaces deep inside filled only with fear and frustration. We rarely hear words that draw our soul into the soul of another human being and, together, into God.

~ Dr. Larry Crabb

On the next night of viewing, a second tunnel of uniformed fireman greeted us in the foyer, barricading yet another mass of people waiting to share their condolences.

I had heard the man responsible for Ben's accident wanted to come to the viewing. After his immediate arrest at the scene, he had spent one night in jail and his in-laws posted the bail, releasing him on Monday. Apparently he was distraught and riddled with guilt, but when my nephew Jason asked if I wanted to see the man who had caused Ben's death, I told him no.

I did not want to know what he looked like. *I didn't want to have a face, a picture or a fear.* I wanted to be able to sit at a restaurant with him in the booth behind me and not know he was Ben's killer. I didn't want to be looking for him everywhere I went, wondering if he would run into me. Both nights, the policemen put guards outside the funeral home. They had his picture in case he decided to show up and assured us they would not let him through the door. I never knew if he came.

By this time, I was over-whelmed and borderline delirious. If I heard one more person give me a ridiculous sympathy or explanation of why Ben had died, I was going to slap somebody. Then my favorite daughter-in-law and I devised a plan to deal with the idiotic people, keeping what was left of my sanity intact.

Whenever someone used a line like, "You're such a mighty woman of God that he wanted you all to himself", "Ben's in a better place now" or "This is part of God's plan and all things work together for good", I pulled open the lever to the hidden trap door beneath them. I would smile, shaking their hand with my right arm. As soon as they said something ridiculous, I'd "chi-chunk" with my left arm. By pulling on the pretend secret lever, I'd picture them disappearing down the black hole, as their terrified screaming slowly faded away. The imaginary trap door was genius and worked wonders, helping me survive the second evening after sending at least a hundred people, with Karen's help, to their sudden demise.

The morning of the funeral, I forced myself out of bed and went into the bathroom. When I came back into my bedroom, there stood my two friends and sister again. I stopped in my tracks.

"What the hell are y'all doing here so early for?" I whined loudly. The three of them faced me, holding their ground as if we were preparing for a dual.

"We came to help you get ready," they said carefully and nodded towards the bed. I followed their line of sight and lying on my bed was a gray, wool, three-piece-suite with a black blouse tucked inside.

"No I'm not wearing that. I haven't worn anything like that in ten years!" I exclaimed firmly, pointing at the hideous ensemble in front of me, "It looks like death. If I have to wear a suit, I'm wearing a red blouse. Ben would want me in red today. I have to wear red."

The traditional Southern Baptist widow enrobed in black I had seen through the years was glaring in my mind again. I'd be damned if I looked like that stereotype. I was wearing red. They tried talking me out if it, but I wouldn't budge. Eventually they let me have my way. I picked out a navy blue suit, sporting my ruffled red blouse underneath.

While I finished getting ready, I remembered having to choose the last outfit I would ever pick out for Ben. We had a dilemma about the clothes because his parents wanted him in a formal suit, being that it was the proper way, but I wanted him in his Maui Harley shirt and jeans. Whenever he visited a new town, he found the local Harley shop and purchased a black t-shirt. Maui, Hawaii had been our last vacation. However, out of respect for my in-laws, I reluctantly caved to their wishes. Ben would be laid to rest in a stuffy, navy blue suit Granny had bought with his t-shirt I had folded and set across his chest.

I couldn't believe I had to have a conversation about how to dress my husband for his burial. Every step and each decision in the funeral and burial processes were so foreign and difficult to comprehend. My cognizance had died with Ben, disconnecting me from reality, and I was just going through the motions. I had to keep reminding myself that all of this was actually happening, and *it was happening to me*. It wasn't someone else's trauma, or a counselee's grievous life story. This would forever be part of my history.

I felt crippled by the unexpected severance, as if I had lost a part of me, like an arm or a leg, something should be missing. But when I looked down, my body was still whole. I was still alone.

The sun was shining brightly as it had the entire week. I hated the light and the warmth and the life it represented, as if it too decided to join the masses in trying to force-feed me false hope. *How dare the sun not cooperate with my mood and show its face on a day like today?*

We pulled into the funeral home parking lot once again. I felt like I had lived in this awful, morbid place the past three days. Policemen were directing traffic for the crowds that were gathering, and the fire department brought out their ladder trucks to shut down the main road. The director led us in through the back door for the final private family viewing.

When Pop, Granny and Ben's side of the family took their turns saying good-bye, Pop leaned over his casket and started wailing, "You are my favorite, you are my favorite!", in front of everybody, including his other two sons standing right beside him. "You are my right hand! I love the others, but you are my favorite!" He screamed again and again at the top of his lungs. I wanted to die for Ben's brothers as they held their father, listening to the uncensored truth pour out of him.

Several minutes later, Ben's family was escorted into another room to give our family time alone with Ben. I watched each member surround Ben in somber silence. Our brother-in-law Doug began crying, clenched his fists and angrily started beating Ben's lifeless chest.

"I was supposed to go before you! You're supposed to look after my family. I'm not supposed to look after yours," he shouted through his tears, violently shaking the coffin. My nephews rushed to Doug's side and pulled him away from Ben, and then everybody fell apart.

I just stared in disbelief at the heartbreaking scene playing out before me until the tears blurred my vision. I didn't take any time alone with Ben and I couldn't touch him or kiss him good-bye like the others. I was afraid his body would shatter if I touched him. My husband was dead; I couldn't do it.

After a few more agonizing minutes passed, my other brother-in-law gathered us together and we joined hands in a circle. "Every one of you look at them now," he summoned, as all eyes turned to Josh, Dusty and I. "Pledge that you will honor them and help them in any way possible. This is what Ben would want."

Then we lifted our hands up in one accord and emphatically cheered, "All for one and one for all!" A tiny smile crept across my face at the thought of people hearing us outside the room, probably thinking we were crazy; I liked it.

The chapel inside the funeral home was jam-packed. Uniformed fireman lined the entire wall on one side and the over-flow stood at the back of the chapel, or out into the foyer and hallways. I was ushered to the front wooden pew with my sons and we took our seats. Giant flower arrangements adorned the pulpit area and filled the stage.

John, our pastor and Ben's good friend, opened the service with the passage from 2 Corinthians 4 about the earthen vessels and a verse from Luke that my niece had shared with me earlier in the week. Then Jason took over and began by introducing our nephew Matt. A thunder of applause erupted as Matt stood, tears flowing down his face and that was the first time I felt the magnitude of people surrounding us. They had come to celebrate and honor Ben's life, also signifying the hole he had left behind.

I kept thinking Ben would never ever believe in a million years how this city congregated together for him. He had always been a quiet, simple man who did good, not expecting anything in return.

The songs were played that Josh had selected and as the service concluded, we all rose to our feet. They gently rolled Ben's closed casket by us and Dusty reached out, solemnly placing his hand on top as his final good-bye.

A limousine was waiting to drive us to the cemetery and as we pulled out of the parking lot, some of our family in the car beside us had rolled down all the windows, waving the hang-loose sign in memory of Ben.

When the funeral procession began, Josh looked out the window and his eyes widened, "Oh my god, look mom," he said in awe, "they never bring the ladder truck out!"

The four of us looked through the tinted windows and, to our amazement, saw the massive red fire truck blocking the main road for our procession. Firemen were lined up outside as well, even though most of them were off duty today.

We were the first ones to arrive at the cemetery and drove over to the plot I had picked out the other day. The tent and chairs were prepared for us and Dusty walked me to the front, middle seat. I saw the dark barren hole that would soon be filled with my husband and I was terrified.

The reality that *this is it, this is the last stop, Ben will be gone forever and I will never see his face again,* was racing through my head, but I had to press through.

I wanted Ken, the director and founder of Simply Grace and my dear friend, to conduct the graveside service. I had also asked another close friend of Ben's and mine to say a few words.

Briefly scanning the cemetery grounds, I saw cars funneling into the grid of connecting roads. What felt like hours later, everyone finally found a parking spot, using every inch of pavement available, and crowded in around us.

I was shocked at how many people arrived. We normally paid our respects at a viewing or service, but never the actual burial unless it had been immediate family.

Ken waited patiently for everyone to find a place to stand and settle down, and began by addressing the family and me. He challenged them to let me feel what I needed to feel, as long as I needed to feel it, and truly grieve.

He challenged me to receive, because for so many years I gave diligently, but now it was time for me to receive. Which may sound easy for some, but I was prone to extreme stubbornness. I didn't like being needy or having to ask for anything. He encouraged all of us to care for each other and find unity in our pain and grieving.

Then our friend talked about the faith hall of fame in Hebrews where it says "of whom the world is not worthy" and how the world was not worthy of Ben because of everything he did for so many people. He also used the quote I chose from St. Francis of Assisi, "Preach the gospel at all times and, when necessary, use words."

After he concluded with a prayer, a single white dove was released into the air. Usually doves would fly to the nearest tree and return, but this one flew away and didn't come back, leaving in its wake, a single white feather that gently floated to the ground.

When the casket was lowered into the grave, the pallbearers took off their boutonnieres and dropped them down into the dark pit. The cemetery crew promptly appeared, ready to finalize Ben's burial and fill his grave. I couldn't bear to watch as loads of red soil were dumped over my husband. We waited inside the limo instead.

The guests eventually made their way back to their cars and slowly filed out of the cemetery. I looked around the expansive graveyard as we were driven towards the exit, knowing I would be back. Part of me was here now.

In the reception hall at the funeral home, there was a buffet table prepared, but the thought of food made me sick. A woman from our small group had fixed me a plate and set it down in front of me. I glanced at the steaming varieties of casseroles and back at her expectant stare.

"If you put one bite in my mouth," I said firmly, "I'm going to scream." She laughed nervously and said okay while cautiously edging away from the table.

I didn't want to eat, see, or talk to anybody; I just wanted to get out of there and hide in my room. Five minutes later, my nephew Jason politely excused us, thanking everyone for their love and support, and my son drove us home.

Later that night, I was sipping on one of the many screwdrivers to come, when family members started coming through my front door carrying brown paper bags. Liquor bottles, drink mixes, and cocktail glasses covered the kitchen island countertop, and soon after, all of us were shit-faced.

We were sitting around the living room being goofy and I had a sudden urge to dance. I survived this wretched day and wanted to release the dreary doom and gloom by celebrating. "Let's dance. Let's do the electric slide!" I shouted and giggled, "Ben would want us to dance, whaddya think?"

"Yes," Joan said, nodding solemnly, "Yes he would. What should we dance to?"

I stumbled over to the CD stand and John Mellencamp jumped out at me. Eight of us formed a line through the kitchen and family room, blasting his song "Cherry Bomb" while doing the electric slide. I knew Ben would love that his family danced on the night of his funeral. I loved that we could celebrate and laugh together, and for a few fleeting moments, everything felt okay in the world.

Chapter 6

A Widow's Reproach

Religion is for people who are afraid of going to hell. Spirituality is for people who have already been there.
~ Bonnie Raitt

Six weeks had passed since Ben died. I dropped twenty-five pounds, not because I wanted to or even cared, but because grief had stolen my appetite among many other things. I abated everyone's incessant nagging to eat by forcing down a couple Saltine crackers and drinking a small glass of skim milk.

Joan had spent every night with me and each morning when I woke up, there was a glass of water and an Aspirin waiting at my bedside because she knew I would be hung over. Fear kept her by my side constantly. She thought if she stayed with me, then I wouldn't kill myself. One day, both of my sisters, Joan and Faye, came into my bedroom and had found me lying in bed, blankly staring at the opposing wall.

"Let's go out to eat! It's time for you to get out of the house," Faye urged with way too much gusto and pep. "You haven't been out of the house in three weeks. Get up, shower, put on your make-up, fix your hair, and we're coming back to get you."

I sighed loudly in acknowledgement from under the covers and remained in a fetal position until they exited the room. We arrived at the restaurant just before 11:00 am and, while they went to the restroom, the server had approached our table and kindly introduced herself.

"What can I get you to drink this morning? We have Coke, Sprite, Sweet Tea, Lemon-…"

"I'll have two margaritas please," I ordered curtly.

Her eyes widened in surprise, but she quickly recovered with a trained smile, "Starting early are you?"

"Yep," I had said, handing back the food menu she just gave me.

When my sisters came back to our table, I was already guzzling down the first drink. I didn't even have time to look up when Joan said, "Oh my god! Alright. Okay," as she nervously glanced around at the nearby diners, checking to see if anyone had noticed her overly thirsty sister.

"Okay, maybe this was not a good idea," she whispered feverishly, clearly embarrassed, while sliding my drinks towards the center of the table. "Let's go."

They had decided to grab lunch at a drive-thru and I bitched at them the whole way home. If everybody wanted to drag my ass around, insisting on taking me everywhere, then I was going to be drunk doing it.

My friends, family, and colleagues were desperate to do something for me, like it was their way of coping by trying to make me feel better. They wanted the *old* Bekki back, as if this other Bekki was no fun, too depressing, too much to bear. I didn't blame them. The morphing thoughts and beliefs about my faith and God wouldn't fit into other's staunchly protected god boxes anymore. Their shallow, pious convictions couldn't phase the malignant pain and anger of my mourning.

Mail would continuously pour in with cards full of stale sympathies and nauseating religious dribble. I had received gift certificates for massages, mani-pedi sets, aromatherapy baskets and candles, and a-thousand-and-one invitations to go out to eat. I sometimes wondered if sitting at a restaurant was the best consolation people could conjure us, as if a nice meal together was a cure-all, when the thought of eating publically soured my mood.

> Why didn't I receive offers to go out for drinks, or at least to just come over, without agenda or recompense, and sit with me in the uncomfortable silence of my sorrow?

At that time, I couldn't voice their genuine but feeble attempts to comfort me were in vain, that there wasn't anything anyone could do to help. I was on autopilot and all I was really thinking was *I just wanted to die.*

Each day was a fight to survive. I dreaded waking up because I never knew how I could live another day in this desolate hopelessness. I feared going to sleep because night brought with it the crushing waves of sadness, despair, and painful loneliness. The first night I had to spend by myself, I took two sleeping pills, making doubly sure I would stay asleep. I was terrified of waking up alone, afraid that the grief would swallow me whole in the darkness.

I had become fast friends with the prescriptions and thought they complimented my screwdrivers beautifully. I found what worked and stuck with it. I began looking forward to how both would keep me afloat through the bleak and distressful nights. Eventually, Joan became concerned and had tried discouraging my budding habit.

"You can't do this!" She would scold. "You're not supposed to mix pills and alcohol."

"Oh yah?!" I'd snap back daringly, narrowing my eyes at her,

"Watch me." And I would pop the pills in my mouth, followed by the remains of my mixed drink, and swallow the nightcap cocktail in front of her disapproving stare.

Every afternoon at 2:00, Joan would come back to the house and take me on a two-hour car ride because Ben would come home from work at that time and I couldn't handle being there. She would drive everywhere imaginable while I wept in the passenger seat next to her.

Then my daughter-in-law would get home around 4:00 pm. She would come downstairs to check on me and start making her delicious screwdrivers for me. I was fully capable of mixing drinks myself, but that was Karen's way of comforting me. She was also the only one that put salt in the drink, which I loved. Half the time, she sat and drank with me too and let me get smoking pissed the drunker I became.

One friend had cleared her busy schedule to spend the day with me. When I asked her if she was taking the day off for me, or for her, she was honest and said it was for her. I felt how much she needed this time together, so I chose to suck it up, fake my interest and go with her.

She had planned a day at the spa and when we arrived, the receptionist showed me to my room and quietly shut the door behind her. I took off all my clothes, laid chest down, pulled the white linen sheet up to my shoulderblades, and rested my face on the pillowed circle. The masseuse came in shortly after and had begun rubbing my back.

When I felt the touch of someone else's hands on my bare skin, I instantly burst into tears, realizing how much I had missed Ben's hands. Up until that day, I had shied away from anything more than the sympathy hugs, and even then I became a limp noodle with my feeble attempt to return another's embrace. I was in too much pain to let anyone that close.

Like a leaky faucet, I had watched the warm tears slip down my nose, through the face cradle, and disappear into the carpet. I cried silently the entire hour as the deep longing for Ben's touch had been awakened inside me. The way his closeness had made me feel safe, owned, aroused. The ways he had been intimate with me.

The masseuse didn't ask any questions, but I had wondered if she thought I was crazy, or even noticed my muted anguish. Before leaving the room, I tried composing myself by gluing on a semi-happy, relaxed face, and never told my friend how painful the experience had been.

My faithful friend DeeAnn would visit me on Wednesdays. She'd bring her sack lunch and sit in the bedroom with me all day. She would ask if I had eaten yet, or if I had showered, and I would answer no to both questions. Sometimes we would talk and she would listen to me scream, cry, or rail at God, and sometimes we would be silent, and she would sit there while I mindlessly stared at a show on T.V.

I wanted to watch March Madness, an annual tradition with Ben and me, and I had a growing affinity for the evening news. I had never liked the news beforehand because it was too depressing. But now I felt a counterfeit connection to the pain of the world, like it gave me comfort to see other people hurting, and I wasn't the only one barely breathing.

Any tragic event was like an outward expression of my inner pain.

I would sigh in relief when I heard of a bridge collapsing suddenly, or when natural catastrophes like Hurricane Katrina hit and innocent people died. When Steve Irwin "The Crocodile Hunter" died later in the year, I was comforted as I grieved with his wife and family, who were obviously complete strangers that lived halfway around the planet.

DeeAnn had convinced me to come back to Simply Grace, probably to be out amongst the living, and because we were still in the middle of the women's class I had left since Ben died. The first time I went, the women were shocked. They were very supportive and loving but I did not want to be there. While DeeAnn taught, I would sit at the end of the large table thinking how much I didn't care about the women sitting around me.

I had said things in my head at them like, "You know what? You think you have trouble…if y'all knew what I was thinking right now, you wouldn't want to be within fifteen miles of me." I was out for blood, but I kept going every week, silently venting through each class.

There were, on occasion, times I let God in with winced eyes and trembling hands, unsure of what he would do or say, trying to believe he would follow through with his promises.

I would beg him for mercy, mercy, mercy; for some relief from this hell of heartache.

Most days I thought I was dying and wondered if he heard my cries, doubting he cared.

He told me his heart was broken for me…

Then why would you allow this to happen? I demanded.

He said he can and will take care of me…

But when?! I didn't know how much longer I could exist in this darkness and helplessness.

How far would he let me sink?

I thought he was supposed to be *the* comforter, full of compassion and love. But all I could feel was my body and soul slowly bleeding out while he kept his distance, unwilling to jump in and save me.

I avoided everything that reminded me of Ben like the plague. Pictures, mail, phone calls, his family, because any trigger would send me spiraling down the black hole. Many times my sisters found me collapsed on the bathroom, kitchen, or bedroom floor because something had reminded me of Ben. My physical body would buckle from the sudden, intense pain and I would just fall to the ground. I was crippled with grief.

My doctor would call to check on me every now and then, and had suggested that I talk to one of his friends. He gave me her number and, following his orders, I called her a few days later. At first, I had struggled telling someone I had never seen or met what I was going through, but the uneasiness quickly lifted when she told me her husband had died suddenly as well. He had gone out for his routine bike ride and never came home.

I was encouraged listening to her because she had made it through, that two years later, she was still alive. She had started the movement for the road signs that read, "Share the Road." She told me about a group that had helped in her grieving process, and then gave me details and directions. She also wanted to meet me there for my first class.

The thought of being with a group of strangers scared me, but I wanted answers. I was tired of asking the same question "why" over and over. I wanted a lifeline, anything to help me survive. When I had called to sign up, they told me I had to wait three more weeks for the next class to start.

Three weeks? I choked back; *I'm dreading the next three hours. Three weeks is an eternity away!*

In the meantime, I went along with whatever people wanted me to do, which was still mainly going to restaurants. I hated every second of being in public, outside of my comfortable seclusion.

I felt ragged and raw, like anyone who saw me would know what had happened to me; as if they could smell my shame over their steak dinner and think, "Here is the woman God has stricken."

I was ashamed, shamed for being a widow. But I didn't *do* anything; this was something that happened to me. God was the one who cheated on me.

He promised me that he had my back, while hiding a knife behind his. He took away something I believed and trusted in, someone I loved. I had thought God and I knew and understood each other and we were on the same page, like my plan was his plan. *If anything, God should be ashamed. He gave me this weight.*

I felt the residue of my crossbred southern Baptist / Pentecostal beliefs poisoning my thoughts, convincing me that I was being punished. Whenever the pain spiked, I knew somehow it must be my fault. I was paying my due penalty.

> But for what? Hadn't I been obedient and diligent in following what God had shown me? Was becoming a counselor and working full-time as a volunteer staff member not enough for him? What about thirty-one years of being a good, loving wife to Ben, and living a healthy and fulfilling marriage together?

No. God had betrayed me. And I could not understand, for the life of me, why I carried the shame. This was not a part of the "Six Steps to Grieving." It was an unwelcomed guest in the midst of my deep sorrow and pain. It was a nameless, crooked thief in the night that stripped me of what I held dear; left all alone feeling naked and bare everywhere I went, with no end in sight.

Chapter 7

Grief Group Happy Hour

It's not a cry you can hear at night. It's not somebody who has seen the light. It's a cold and it's a broken hallelujah.
~ Leonard Cohen

The firsts and lasts had started soon after Ben's death. The first Valentine's Day apart. The last time we had made love. When I realized I would not be having sex with Ben anymore, another raging tantrum had quickly ensued. I yanked open my drawer of unmentionables, ready to clear out everything inside, but when I saw the lingerie neatly folded and untouched, my anger turned to mourning and dropped me to my knees.

The next ten minutes were spent on the floor sobbing while I delicately handled the beautiful undergarments individually, as a heavy sadness ached from some hidden source inside me. Each piece embodied fond and deeply intimate memories. One I had kept from our honeymoon, representing several decades of marriage, some Ben had purchased for special occasions, and others signified the great sex life we celebrated together.

I had carefully stood back up; slowly wiping the remaining tears from my cheeks and chin with the palm of my hand. I found a tinted garbage bag so no one could see its contents, and as I began stuffing my lingerie inside, the grieving instantly switched back to anger.

Never again! I will never wear these things for my husband again! I will never have sex with Ben again! I had cried, screaming at my pain. *This is pure torture!*

I continued the venting session while stomping out to the garbage bin, furiously whipping all our affectionate memories away, and slammed the lid shut with violent contempt.

My fiftieth birthday had come and went on a dismal, rainy day. I wanted to mope in bed all day and avoid anything remotely happy about my birth. Days like those didn't matter anymore. Why would they if Ben wasn't there to enjoy the special times with me? My sons and daughter-in-law had taken me out to in spite of my melancholic attitude; I may have cracked a few smiles after a few drinks, but I was drowning inside.

The night of my first class was finally here. My sister picked me up after I threw on something other than pajamas and a couple smudges of make-up. The group met in a little old, white Episcopalian church. I was extremely anxious when we pulled into the parking lot and felt fear twisting at my stomach.

As we approached the front door, fresh tears stung my eyes. Before I could try and push the swelling pain away, heaving sobs gushed out of me. I was terrified of this moment. The grief group represented another confirmation that I was doing this because my husband was dead. The reality that I had to live the rest of my life without Ben was still difficult to accept.

I was no longer a couple, half of a whole, a soul mate. I was empty, alone, afraid.

Joan gently took my hand, after dabbing away her own tears, and we walked in together. We went down a flight of stairs, through a children's Sunday school room, and into what seemed like a media room of sorts. I counted six chairs lined up in the shape of a crescent moon, and two chairs set in front for the teachers. The room was cold and dimly lit with fluorescent lights buzzing overhead and smelled like crayons, Elmer's glue, and construction paper.

Once everybody arrived and claimed a seat, our teachers introduced themselves. They both had spouses that died and they had met each other several years ago in this class. Apparently there was an unspoken rule about not getting into a relationship with fellow students, but they did anyway and were now married. Then it was our turns. Each person stated their name and plainly proceeded to explain the heartbreaking stories of how they were widowed.

When it was my turn to share, all I really wanted to say was, "Hi. My name is Bekki. And God fucked me over too.", but I refrained and used my polite version instead. After I finished talking, there was a long, silent pause until the teacher looked at me and sincerely said, "You're going to live that day over again."

"You'll *have* to."

I thought he was out of his mind. There was no way I was going back to the day from hell.

> Who was he to tell me what I would or wouldn't do? And why didn't he say that to anybody else? Had they already relived the worst day imaginable?

I was surprised to hear everyone had experienced the death of a spouse. Some had sudden deaths like Ben's; some had drawn out deaths due to illness or cancer. We talked about which kind would be worse: If you knew your spouse was going to die and had to watch the terrible process, but also had that time to prepare yourself. Or, if your spouse instantly died, and you not only had to deal with shock and denial, but also the pain of their sudden death.

I wondered if some were searching for their last good-bye like me. I was frustrated I had not yet found one. Sometimes I doubted if a good-bye even existed, or if it was too much to ask, too soon.

> Was it left suspended in mid-air, waiting for me to catch it? Was God dangling Ben's farewell in front of my nose?

I felt that this basement was the saddest place on earth, like AA but more depressing. At least addicts had hope. They could look forward to a string of sober days, gaining some semblance of consistency.

The grievers just got together and grieved, coping as best we knew how with the unknown. Like maybe one day I would feel a little better, perhaps even notice the sun was shining, then the next day I would be bed-ridden from the paralyzing deep grief. I felt schizophrenic, but was comforted in hearing some of these people had similar experiences.

When the class ended, we all received workbooks to take home and were assigned certain pages of questions and journal exercises to complete for next week. The husband-wife teachers went around and hugged each of us, and as she reached out to hug me, a pungent waft of alcohol met my nose.

My teacher reeked of a brewery. Like she had snuck off to a darkened corner or empty single bathroom nearby and, reaching into her purse with shaky, fiendish hands, fished out her flask of Jack, sucked down several gulps as her lips curl with the tiniest smile of relief.

I ignored the formidable scent, returning her embrace, and Joan and I left in contemplative silence. On the ride home, all I thought about was the teacher. I didn't care how much or how often she drank, because I was doing the same thing in that respect, but the fact that she came tipsy to class freaked me out. As if I was staring at one of those images that tested a child's comprehensive skills and asked: What's wrong with this picture?

This woman, our leader, was telling us not to cope with our grief by using pills, drugs, or alcohol out of one side of her mouth, while drinking from the other. Years had passed since her husbands' death, but she couldn't make it through a two-hour class sober? I was stunned and a bit unsettled.

The razor-thin sliver of hope I had let in since Ben's death was quickly fading. There was that elusive word again; hope. *Will it ever be real in my life?* I thought I knew what it was, or just mixed it in with the other religious buzzword, faith.

I remembered the morning after Ben had died when I was dazedly sitting in my room alone and my niece came in to visit. I noticed Kassie was carrying something small in her hand as she sat down beside me on the bed.

"Kristy gave this to me when we lost Abigail," she had said quietly, while opening her hand revealing a simple, silver ring with a bold inscription lining the outside. "I know this belongs to you now. I want to give it to you." She gestured for me to take the ring and as I did, I saw the word was "Hope".

Hope, I thought angrily to myself. *It's too late to hope. He's dead!* I didn't know what to hope for or hope in. God could not be trusted. Hope meant nothing to me. If anything, it was a curse, a bitter reminder of my desolate despair.

My husband was six feet under ground and I was ready to join him. Not only had I purchased the burial plot next to him for when I died, but I also had a marked grave waiting for me. When I picked out Ben's headstone, I had my name and birthday inscribed on the right side of my husband's memorial. All the family had to do was fill in the date of my death.

Joan had tried persuading me otherwise, telling me to think of my children and how my decision would scare them, but I told her to shut up and leave me alone. I couldn't imagine living much longer. She replied by calling me a dumbass.

My sister and I continued going to grief group together and I would complete my homework like I had to turn it in; meaning, I was never as honest on paper as I was really feeling. I attended the class because I felt a comforting comradery here. I had found solace in these people and their pain.

One night after the session was over, one of the women approached me, staring at me squarely, leaning in uncomfortably close to my face.

"Whatever you do," she said affectionately, "Walk. No matter what the weather's like, dress accordingly, get out and walk. Every day you walk. No matter what happens."

I took her advice to heart and the next morning I walked. I walked every day since then. I would bundle up, or grab an umbrella, take the dog and out we went. The time outside gave me a chance to get away from the cave-dwelling and clear my head; it became my mini-reprieve from the monotonous nightmare of grieving.

Even if my newfound walking ritual was the only thing I accomplished in twenty-four hours besides maybe brushing my teeth, then, at the very least, I had survived another day.

The first of April arrived bringing a restlessness that made me uneasy. I was still living in the same house Ben and I had been together in, and now, the agonizing emptiness of that space was suffocating me.

I was thankful for Josh and Karen's company, and they had helped me through many dark hours, but that was not enough anymore. I needed to escape and catch my breath but I didn't know how.

Last October, Ben had started re-building a house nearby and was adamant about making sure I had a key to the house. I questioned him and told him I didn't need it for anything, but he wanted me to have that key. Ben loved construction and had purchased a few houses with the intention of flipping them. Now, of course, they were left undone.

Dusty also shared that passion and had recently moved into the unfinished home and continued the remodeling. He began telling me whenever I wanted to get out; he would help me move that day. At first, his suggestion felt daunting, as if a relocation would be too intrusive on my mind and body, but now it sounded more appealing.

One morning, I was already having a particularly hard day. I woke up angry and needed some space, so I grabbed the spare key and drove over to the unfinished house. When I opened the front door, the sun's bright yellow rays were bursting through the large living room windows.

I walked across the soft, carpeted floor and laid down in front of the barren fireplace. As an ambushing flood of emotions swept over me, I curled up into a tight ball and broke down sobbing from the sudden swell. I was frustrated, mad, depressed, and felt completely helpless and alone. I cried to God, begging him for guidance. I had so many questions. So many things left unresolved and up in the air.

I felt like I had abandoned Simply Grace, my counselees, my students, friends, and co-workers. I felt stagnant after being so busy for so long, as if I needed to be doing something. *I wasn't used to feeling useless*; but I wasn't ready to go back. I could barely sit through a few hours of our weekly women's class.

I was also concerned about my finances. Ben worked for the government and as soon as the office heard Ben had died, they followed protocol and contacted our bank. The bank immediately froze our accounts, savings, assets, retirement, life insurance, even his last paycheck.

I was supposed to be drawing survivor's benefits right away as well, but in order to receive the benefits; I was required to produce a death certificate. However, the official toxicology reports were needed just to get the certificate. When we went to the Georgia Bureau of Investigations asking for the proper paperwork, they would not release Ben's reports.

I was livid. Ben was dead and buried. Why couldn't they hand over his reports? All of my funds had been frozen and the bank management would not budge. They strictly enforced the mandated procedures because it protected them from fraud, but I wasn't trying to scam anybody; I was trying to survive.

Finally, a nice woman from the Victim's Rights Advocacy called, after I had stormed their office, torch and pitchfork in-hand, and passed out a few sound, verbal lashings. She explained that I was considered a victim of crime and they were working on my case; but nothing had happened yet. So what was the hold up?

Dusty had jumped in to help and took over the responsibilities. He dealt with the post office, bank and GBI. Then my brother-in-law showed up in my driveway one day and had asked me to come sit in the truck with him. He told me the night after Ben died, he had a dream with Ben telling him to take care of his family.

At the time, Doug didn't know what taking care of us would look like; but apparently, as he handed me a large check, he had figured it out. He said the money was a gift. I was never to repay him and to let him know if I needed more. Luckily, we didn't have any debt or unpaid bills, but I did have car payments, utility costs, and basic living expenses. I knew, thanks to Doug's contribution, I could breathe a little easier while I waited for the financial mess to clear.

I held the check with acceptance and gratitude, but my thoughts had quickly fixated on Doug's dream.

> How had he seen Ben so soon? Would I ever dream of Ben or would I even want to? I was desperate to see him just one last time, but was it worth having to watch him leave me behind again?

As I continued crying on the living room floor, hugging my knees into my chest and releasing some of my frustration, I told God I didn't know what to do. I was tired, over-whelmed and felt stuck and powerless. My helpmeet wasn't here to make decisions with me; I wasn't used to feeling so debilitated. Depending on God with my daily life was abnormal and scared me at times.

> Did he even care about these mundane details? Did he really have my best interest in mind?

Then, like he had snuck in through the back door and sat down on the stone hearth beside me, he interjected my train of thought and simply said, "Move. Move here."

I instantly stopped crying, sat straight up and quietly looked around the empty, silent house, surprised by his direct response.

Was it crazy to move into a new home at a time like this, just three months after my husband's death? Could I handle being even more alone than I was already? Obviously God wanted me here, but what if he's setting me up?

Chapter 8

Red Birds & Grey Goose

Shot through the heart and you're to blame;
you give love a bad name. I play my part and
you play your game; you give love a bad name.
~ Jon Bon Jovi

Late one morning, I was sipping some coffee and watching the news, and I could hear voices and movement coming from upstairs. Soon after, I heard footsteps racing down the stairs and Karen's voice. "Bek!" My daughter-in-law called frantically, flinging the door open abruptly.

"Yah, I'm here." I answered from my bedroom as she stepped through the doorway. "Why aren't you at work? Who's upstairs with you?"

She paused, taking a deep breath as if she was about to deliver a momentous speech. "Well, the family came to be with you today."

Okay, I thought while studying her face intently, noticing her eyes and nose looked red. She seemed nervous and sad.

"Why do they need to be with me?" I asked warily. Small glints of pain flickered in her eyes, but her voice and demeanor remained strong.

"Ben didn't die from the impact of the accident." She said slowly and with great deliberation. Another deep breath.

"He died…because the flight crew messed up." She finished,

almost sighing with relief that the news was out in the open and off her chest. I blinked. My brain froze and my heart dropped, again. *What does that mean?*

"Karen…" I responded carefully, afraid of what would come next. "*What* did they mess up?!"

She sat down beside me, still trying to keep her emotions in check while she began relaying the facts. I tried keeping up with the order of events and technical terms, but a second cycle of shock and denial slowed my comprehension abilities as she talked.

When Ben was hit, he had been knocked unconscious momentarily, but was coherent again by the time the first responders arrived. However, he kept asking the team what had happened as they were stabilizing him. The paramedics discerned his repetitive questioning was evidence of head trauma and radioed in the accident for air flight support.

Twenty minutes later, the helicopter had landed and, because the flight crew had more medical training than the paramedics, they took command of the scene. When my husband was assessed, he had two cracked ribs and a headache. But the flight nurse thought his condition was severe enough to intubate and fly him to the hospital; which meant Ben had to be sedated.

Ben was given the anesthesia and when intubation had begun, the tube went down his esophagus instead of the trachea, which would only pump air into his stomach. After they discovered the first attempt was unsuccessful, they had to remove the tube and try again. The second attempt was successful, and by this time, Ben's oxygen levels had dropped. He was dying.

The head paramedic knew what was happening to Ben and pulled rank on the flight crew, telling them that his team needed to get

Ben to the hospital immediately. *Ben had already died.*

The initial power struggle began when the paramedics had told the flight crew Ben was breathing on his own and he was stable enough for a short ambulance ride. The flight crew disagreed and decided that because they had been called to the scene, they were going to intubate and air flight Ben anyway. They proceeded with a Rapid Sequence Intubation, which was a controversial technique that allowed sixty seconds to establish an airway.

They had obviously taken longer than the allotted minute, and because Ben was sedated, he didn't have the natural gag reflex or any way of letting the crews know he was suffocating. In any emergency situation, every responder is aware that they have one hour, also known as the "Golden Hour", to transport the victim to the nearest hospital and under a doctor's care. Not only was time wasted trying to perform an unnecessary and lethal intubation, but they also could have taken Ben directly to the hospital in ten minutes or less, instead of waiting for the helicopter.

Another problem was that the closest hospital had diverted the initial call for Ben's accident, saying their emergency facility was understaffed. However, a hospital cannot refuse a patient once they are presented. Considering all of the surrounding issues, Ben still ended up riding in the ambulance. He was taken to the same hospital that had tried diverting him. But he was killed at the hands of a power-tripping flight nurse.

When Karen had finished talking, I realized I was holding my breath. I exhaled slowly, feeling completely defeated. Whatever ground I thought I had gained instantly fell out from under me as hot tears began pouring down my cheeks.

No. Not now! Not again. Please not again! I screamed in silent protest.

I cannot take any more. I can't do it! This is the end of me. I'm going to die!

Josh and Dusty came down a few minutes later and saw me weeping. They carefully sat down on either side of me and quietly consoled their despairing mother. While my daughter-in-law left to grab the vodka, my sons explained that an investigation was underway and other details concerning the crime they had been working on since Ben's death. No one wanted to tell me the truth until it was one hundred percent confirmed Ben had not died from the impact. Josh and Dusty needed to break the news today because I had to start signing papers for a wrongful death suit.

I tried listening as they continued describing the legal process and new facts they were discovering, but I wasn't absorbing any information. My head was swimming in shock and extreme anger.

As if the past three months haven't been hard enough trying to accept the death of my husband? Now, right now, I find out Ben was murdered?

With crews of fireman, paramedics, flight nurses, every kind of trained, experienced medical professional right at his fingertips, three hospitals in an eight mile radius; and he was killed…because of a power struggle?!

The Grey Goose was automatically handed to me and I chugged down a few shots. When I felt my menacing nerves had been somewhat relieved from the alcohol, I headed upstairs to sit outside on the front porch.

One by one, more family members started arriving, some carrying deli trays, others carrying brown paper bags. They were coming to mourn with me, all over again. Joan sat next to me as I stared despondently into the front yard, remembering what my grief group teacher had told me in the first class. I looked over at my sister and said sadly, "Do you remember Joan? He told me this would happen, and now it's here."

She looked back at me with her teary eyes and pink, blotchy cheeks. "Yah, I do."

"This is the day. I'm reliving it, just like he said I would!" I cried, stunned by the surreal scene before me. The same cars filled the driveway, same people, house, porch, the sun was shining, and the temperature was warm; exactly like the day when Ben had died.

"I know," she responded softly, knowingly.

I stayed out on the porch for a while and people would come to talk or check on me, but I wasn't present. I was far away, wandering what could possibly be keeping me alive.

Why doesn't he just let me die?

I honestly thought God was trying to kill me at his leisure. While coolly French inhaling the last hit of his cigarette, with the faintest hint of pleasure curling at his lips, he was twisting the knife deep into my back just for good measure.

"He's trying to kill me!" I shrieked loudly, closing my eyes tightly shut, trying to block out the horrifying pain. "He's up there watching me die a slow death and loving every minute of it. He's trying to kill me!"

"No Bekki," came Doug's quiet, calming voice beside me.

"No!" I shouted in defiance. "I can't live through this. I can't!"

I felt the anger raging inside me. "Fine. You know what God; do it! Just finish the job. Please! Do it!"

If he wanted me dead, I was ready. I didn't care anymore. I couldn't keep living this way.

"You son of a bitch!" I screamed furiously at the sky, "Do it!"

"He's not trying to kill you Bek," Doug pleaded back, as the gentle confidence of his voice contrasted with my angry threats still lingering in the spring air, breaking through my fitful rage.

I slowly opened my eyes and saw the pain in Doug's face. He looked so tired and worn. He had been involved with Ben's case too, carrying the truth that his brother-in-law and best friend was murdered. Something about the brokenness in Doug's eyes sobered my consuming wrath. Turning my accusatory gaze back to the front yard, I quieted down and brooded silently in my chair.

"Okay. *God*," I wagered out loud in a less abrasive tone. If he cared about me at all, I wanted proof. "If you are not trying to kill me, I want to see a red bird right here, right now." I said with satisfaction.

Of all the hours spent bird watching, I had never seen a red bird anywhere near this house. I knew my challenge would prove the bastard wrong. However, no sooner did the words leave my mouth, as if my breath itself had taken wings and developed into form, when a brilliantly red Cardinal gracefully flew past the porch into the pine tree next to us, landing assertively on an outer limb in plain view.

"There he is!" Doug gasped in awe. He stood up and walked to the edge of the porch, squinting at the winged sign from above in disbelief.

The Cardinal remained proudly perched on the branch, puffing up his scarlet-feathered chest and stared me dead in the eyes, as if to say, "See, I told you."

I stayed seated in the chair, smugly cocked my head towards the opposite direction, and snuffed in resignation.

Now you're patronizing me? I asked God. *Well, two can play at that game, bud. I'll show you how I don't need you.*

By 4:00 that afternoon, I was plastered along with the rest of our family, but this time, there weren't any drunken laughs, jokes, or reminiscing like the night after Ben's funeral. The mood was depressing and hushed with somber sadness.

Later on, I traipsed down the stairs alone to my bedroom, very drunk and exhausted, and clumsily grabbed for the prescription bottle. After swallowing a few pills, I fell into bed not wanting to wake up ever again, and quickly blacked out.

Tuesday morning dawned as a rank smell met my nose and woke me up. I looked around without moving my head and saw vomit ripening on the pillow and sheets just inches from my face. I sighed irritably and rolled away from the puke.

Still lying in bed, I remembered the first time I woke up in bile, gagging on the throw up that hadn't made it out of my mouth. When I realized what I had been laying in, I was too drunk to care, too pissed to move, too wounded to want to live.

"Why don't you just let me die already?" I had told God, thinking I could have easily slipped away forever by suffocating on my own vomit, but he wouldn't let that happen. He had responded with two words, "Roll over." And I did. I rolled over and fell back asleep with puddles of puke sitting beside me. He was so gentle and patient with me, even though I hated him.

> Was he being this way to keep me healthy enough, alive enough, so I could feel the pain to its fullest extent? Could God be that sadistic?

I felt crazy. I didn't know how to feel. Most days I was giving him the finger with one hand and beckoning him to come hold me with the other. I had heard of wrongful death cases and watched them on drama T.V. shows or movies, but never in our family. Not to me, not Ben. Not from a minor injury of two cracked ribs, with three hospitals just minutes away, and teams of medical professionals at Ben's side.

I could rationalize a car and motorcycle accident, I understood his death in that light. However, a homicide was a whole other beast, it didn't make any sense, it had to be God. The betrayal I felt with him before this new knowledge, paled in comparison to the furious anger growing inside me now.

God was the one that did this, he had allowed Ben to die, and I hated him for it. Yet, he was the only one who could walk me through this unbearable pain and heal me, and I hated him for that, especially now.

After yesterday's event, I spent most of today in bed trying to process the awful truth, toggling between homicidal rage and suicidal despair. I was bloodthirsty. I wanted to find the persons responsible for killing Ben and sue them off the face of the earth. I didn't want them touching another human being or destroying another family the way they had ours.

Then the terrifying darkness of grief would consume my being, like I was caught in a deep well. The water was up to my chin. I was helpless to stop it as I watched the water slowly creeping over my head. I couldn't see the light, an end to this misery. I didn't know if I could ever feel life again.

My family would come in to check on me like they always did, asking me to eat something, shower, or show the basic signs of existence. I ignored them as best as I could and stayed in bed for three more days. On the second morning, my fiery friend Reba showed up and marched into my room again, just like she had done the first few days after Ben died.

"Bek, you'd better eat this or I'm gonna beat your ass!" She sounded off, holding up a lunch she had prepared for me from home. I matched her cavalier attempt with an equally defiant counter.

"The hell I'm not." I answered. "You're not going to make me eat anything. I'm not hungry."

I watched her good-natured, (occasionally over-bearing) maternal constitution dial down a few notches as she lowered the sack lunch.

"Well," she huffed, turning around and stubbornly pacing into the kitchen, "You're gonna eat *something*."

Ten minutes later she was back in my room, positioning the T.V. tray in front of me, and setting a steaming bowl of soup with Saltine crackers on top. I conceded by sipping several spoonfuls of broth just to shut her up.

Joan persistently remained by my side the entire week because I was in too much pain to function in the every day. She cleaned, cooked for my sons, Karen and Katie, ran loads of laundry, and basically became the main caregiver for my family.

At weeks end, I had thoughtfully narrowed down my options on how I was going to proceed with life and God. *If* he truly was the only one who could shoulder all of my pain and anger and, *if* he meant what he said about putting everything on him, then I was going to push him hard.

This was war.

Chapter 9

The Great Purge

Suffering can do that to us...We're forced to imagine a new future because the one we were planning on is gone.

~ *Rob Bell*

Another week crawled by and I felt increasingly trapped. I hadn't told my son and daughter-in-law about my decision to move because of the news concerning Ben and my emotional tailspin afterwards. But now it was time. I saw Ben everywhere in this house and it was smothering me.

That evening, Josh and Karen came downstairs to keep me company as usual and I broke the news to them. Josh was supportive and wanted me to do whatever I thought was best, and Karen took my decision very hard. She was concerned about me and felt that as long as I was under their roof, then she could keep an eye on me. She could monitor me and make sure I wouldn't sneak off and kill myself.

I understood her concerns and fears. Besides the usual 4:00 pm through 11:00 pm alcohol and pill consumption, my concealed drinking had steadily progressed. I was a grown woman hiding liquor bottles under my bed and in the headboard cabinets, trying to avoid further confrontations about my habits. But all I had really wanted was to drink more without the watchful eyes of my sisters. During the sober hours, I was more aware and felt the extent of my pain. I would watch myself, like an out-of-body experience, as God came in, picked me up off the floor, and carried me through the fire (never taking me out of it of course). But in the drunken hours, God would get louder, like he was calling and pleading for me, and I felt more raw and real with him. So then I would drink even more to drown him out and scream back, "Don't you dare sit there and try to tell me you love me!"

I had to get out of that basement. I told Karen I would be okay, this was my choice, and it was a good thing. I needed to move on and I had to let her be sad. I needed this for me.

The following week, my sister came over early in the morning to help with the move. I think she was there more for moral support, because after about two minutes of packing, I went ballistic. I saw the things Ben and I had shared, so many memories attached to them and I hated all of it, especially the kitchen items. Plates, spatulas, Crock-Pots, cookie tins, fry pans, woks, blenders, the toaster, everything went. I threw it all away.

Joan watched me clearing out the cupboards and warned with a furrowed brow, "Bek, You're gonna need this stuff."

"Nope." I snapped, purposely ignoring her demanding stare as I continued filling the trash cans. I threw away cookbooks marked with all of Ben's favorite recipes, mixing bowls, casserole dishes, pots, cake pans, cups, wooden spoons. I didn't need them anymore. I would never cook or bake for him again; I couldn't stand any of it. I had already gotten rid of Ben's things soon after he died. I was in another drunken frenzy and stripped my husband's dresser and closet bare.

I had thrown all of his clothes in the trunk, except for his motorcycle gear, and my ever present designated driver Joan took me over to Goodwill. I had questioned myself on the ride there. My mom had kept dad's stuff in the closet for a year, and other's I knew who took even longer trying to let go of their spouse's belongings.

> Was this too soon and, if so, did it look like I didn't love Ben, just giving all of his clothes away like this? Why was I second-guessing everything? Was something wrong with my rogue widowhood, or was *I* wrong?

As we neared the Goodwill, I had concluded that because I was in so much pain, I wanted to get everything that was painful dealt with right away, like ripping off the Band-Aids.

I wanted to feel what I needed to feel, but in doing so, I was still trying to play God. *I was still trying to control my healing.*

When we pulled up to the drop-off dock, a friendly round man pushing a shopping cart had come out to greet us. He unloaded everything from our trunk with an amazing quickness, and after he finished, he asked if I wanted a receipt. I told him no.

My sister and I both thanked him and as we drove away, I broke down sobbing. I had felt horrible knowing I was leaving part of me there, just another reminder that Ben was not on planet earth anymore, and to this day, I won't go near a Goodwill.

I scanned the remains in the other rooms of my home. I didn't want our bed or the bedroom suite, and threw away all of our sheets and linens. I couldn't take any of the dining or living room furniture either. By the time I was done ridding the basement apartment of most everything we had owned, moving was really easy.

I showed up at my new house with my clothes and a few pieces of furniture originally purchased for the mountain house Ben and I had planned to build. I felt like I should've been proud of myself for brazenly forging ahead into uncharted territory, or taking the initiative to improve my circumstances; but I was miserable.

I was saying good-bye to another shattered dream of Ben and I escaping away and growing old together in our dream house. I was nineteen years old when Ben and I had married and moved into our own home. I never thought I would be doing this alone; I was too young.

Who does this? I wondered. I remembered the elderly blue-haired widows I had seen growing up who lined the front pews in church sanctuaries. Biding their time in the same house where their spouse had once lived, slowly wasting away like their fantasies of being together forever.

No! I stomped indignantly. *That won't happen to me. I refuse to be like that.*

As I stood alone in the empty foyer, I made up my mind to defy the typical life and image of widowhood. None of this was coming back to bite me in the ass ten years from now. I was going to get *better*, not *bitter*.

After my moving helpers Josh and Joan went home, I headed straight into the kitchen for the alcohol. I made sure my other son Dusty was gone for the night, so I could drink heavily without him knowing. I had learned what hit me faster than my preferred vodka, and today it was whiskey and Coke.

They had set up my new bedroom suite and the only other items in my room at the moment were the T.V. and stand and a tan recliner. I plopped myself down onto the new bed facing the television, turned on the local five o'clock news, and drank another night away.

The next afternoon, I sulked in my chair with a pounding headache and a heavy heart. I had felt ill all morning, not just from the hangover, but I was especially saddened. *Isn't this supposed to be fun and exciting, having my own place?* Then I realized where it was coming from.

I felt exactly the same as I did in the other house. I thought I was supposed to feel better, that moving was going to help, but it didn't. The pain had followed me. I made a geographical change, but the agony was still here, and this was just a different place to grieve.

Chapter 10

Daily Quiet Times

God whispers to us in our pain, speaks to us in our conscience, shouts in our plans. Pain is his megaphone to a rouse a deaf world.
~ C.S. Lewis

Autumn rolled around with all of its flaming colors and grandeur, accompanied by refreshingly cooler breezes that shooed away the never-ending oppressive southern summers. Some trees had already shed their robes of many colors, standing unabashedly exposed against the gentle sun, still sparing a few stubborn leaves desperately holding on for dear life, just like me.

I hated the reminders that time was passing by and I was powerless against it. Like I was stuck in a holding cell or time warp, watching life carry on as usual right in front of me, unable to participate in or experience anything new. *I couldn't live in the present tense.*

My days were spent watching the clock and the calendar, trying to exist by the one thing that remained constant while giving me a false sense of control: time. I had never been a time-oriented person and it was foreign for me to be surviving by the clock. I had always been out living and enjoying life. People would tell me I was the most alive person they had ever met. I had never thought twice about what those compliments meant.

Now I wondered where that woman went and frequently questioned my identity and purpose.

If I wasn't a wife, counselor, or a partner anymore, than who was I? Did my passion, purpose, and identity die alongside Ben? Would I ever feel something other than this over-whelming despair? *What earthly good was I to anybody?*

I had found a place to work out my frustrations. A brand new YMCA had opened in our neighborhood and I quickly signed up for a membership. Abandoning my walking routine, I took to running. Every day I ran on that treadmill for miles. The sight of my sweat hitting the floor made me run even faster and harder; it was a high for me, like I could inflict as much pain on myself as I wanted because I was at a gym. Didn't they expect me to work out really hard?

I loved the Y; it became an escape. I could hide out here, out of sight from my paranoid neighbors who, I was convinced, were gossiping about the crazy widow woman next door that only came outside to exercise her problems away. While behind closed doors, I figured if I could hold off on the drinking until 4:00 pm, and eventually my other pills at bedtime, then I would not be considered an addict. This became my primary illusion of control.

I would get mad at God. I *loved* hating him. I had abided by the other extreme of "living for Jesus", but now just hearing that phrase added insult to injury. I wanted to hurt him like he had hurt me. I thought the best way to do that was to doubt him, doubt his existence. I dabbled in atheism and, for a while, it served me well.

> What kind of god, who I had been taught was a loving and caring being, would allow me to suffer so greatly? Why would he allow the worst thing imaginable to happen in my life, *happen*? He had promised he would not give me more than I could bear, then why this weight?

Everyone had a religious answer or a divine word from the Lord that seemingly comforted their minds or rationalized away their own pain. Then, because it was their rightful duty, they passed it along to me. They were trying to *defend* God, create excuses for him, and over-spiritualize Ben's death. In doing so, my thoughts and feelings had been invalidated, and I was being spiritually abused.

I was completely undone. My life destroyed. The shiny, cookie-cutter solutions couldn't penetrate the deep-seeded doubt that shattered my soul's foundation. We both knew I was not about to defend this monster or make up flaky excuses for his actions.

> Why would the all-knowing, omnipotent one want defense? Why were people so afraid to let him stand up for himself? As if he needed their justifications.

I had checked the reports. I knew exactly what I was doing when the accident happened. At 12:20 pm that Sunday Ben had been hit while I was finishing the retreat with the devotion God gave me.

I was an ordained minister of God, a trained counselor and teacher. *I was teaching women about treasuring their husbands and marriages when he took and ended mine.*

It was ludicrous. I shunned the slightest hint of religion and the law-based remains of pious programming in me. I had burned my ordination certificate and vowed to never counsel married couples or pre-marital couples again. I tried hiding my pain and anger from my family, but my sister would remind me not to stuff my feelings because they were grieving too. However, I didn't let them see the extent of how I coped with the grief.

My sister would still come by and take me out for afternoon drives. Some days I would look up at the car ceiling with tears streaming down my face and yell, "I hate you! I hate you God!", over and over. Afterward, maybe to sugarcoat the depressing ride, Joan would stop at the Dairy Queen drive thru and order us Peanut Buster Parfaits.

At the end of our outings, she would drop me off at my house and I headed straight to the kitchen for my Grey Goose. I never knew that while I started drinking indoors, she would stay parked in my driveway, taking her turn to cry alone before she could go back home.

The investigation for Ben's wrongful death was still unfolding. Dusty had to take responsibility of the lawsuit; because it was obvious I couldn't take care of anything. Josh had decided to step back from the lawsuit because it involved his industry. He didn't want the investigation affecting his crew or his friendships with them.

The man that was booked for vehicular homicide had been released. Our lawyer began subpoenaing the first responders, medics, fireman, and the flight crew, which was a task in itself to find everybody. We found out the cover up had begun the night of Ben's accident, and the news of how he died had spread through the industries and over several counties within three days.

The paramedic who challenged the flight nurse had resigned the next morning after seventeen years of working for his company. Most of the team had quit their jobs and a few others had moved out-of-state soon after.

I began realizing my husband's homicide had turned into a serious case. People literally fled the scene and now they weren't talking. But because I was still in such deep grief, I couldn't process or retain all of the information and details. Dusty would tell me what I needed to know and nothing more. He would say everything three times before his words would register in my head, which soon became an inside joke with the family. If anyone had something important to tell me, they had to repeat it at least three times; otherwise I would forget the message or conversation five minutes later.

The morning of Father's Day I had woken up telling myself I was going to stay wasted the entire day. Not only was it another first without Ben, but it was also Dusty's birthday. A few visitors had the nerve to stop by my house and when they rang the doorbell, I didn't dare answer.

The day of our wedding anniversary had gone by in a drunken haze. I holed up in my bedroom, sobbed for hours in a fetal position on my bed, floor, or chair and tried not to think about another tomorrow. I remembered what my grief group teachers had taught us and I recited it silently through the sorrowful hours, "Survive the Firsts, just survive the Firsts."

One late-October day, I was going through my morning routine; it was a dark day. I woke up in a rage, hung over, feeling terribly alone and was mad at the world and God, again. I had an appointment with our attorney that afternoon. I wanted to stay in bed with the covers over my head the entire day, but I couldn't. I dreaded these meetings. The depositions and fact-finding were way out of my realm, and the minute I stepped out of bed, I was ready to pick a fight.

"Fuck you!" I screamed at God several times over. "I can't do this. *Why* won't you help me?! You never talk to me. Why don't you answer me?!"

I cried on my way to the bathroom, still yelling out obscenities as fast as I could think of them. *Will any of this ever end? Am I doomed to live in this constant state of grief forever?*

I desperately tried to look for a break in the darkness, a silver lining, or a single strand of hope, but I always came back defeated and despairing. He wasn't responding no matter how many times I begged.

Aren't you supposed to be loving and kind, gracious and merciful? Do you care about me at all? I silently shouted in frustration while turning on the shower. Then, as if he had picked me up in the middle of my temper tantrum and sat me down on his knees, he gently said, "Enough."

I froze in mid-stride, immediately quieting my rampant thoughts.

"Shhhhhhhh," he soothed softly, like a father comforting his defiant little girl, "Be tender with me."

Tender? I repeated mockingly. *Be tender with you?* The Lord God Almighty *wants me to be tender with him?*

Although I wanted him to leave me alone, I was secretly intrigued by his request and let him finish what he wanted to say. He had given me permission to drink and take the pills, but not to hurt him or myself any more. And it was time to stop yelling at him whenever the smallest trigger set me off.

Somehow I had readily conceded to God's arrangement as I opened the glass door and stepped into the steaming shower. I felt a new realization weighing into my soul, and my body was buckling from its force. My bare back slid down the wet, fiberglass wall until I was sitting on the shower floor in defeat.

The hot water poured over my head and naked form while I sat under the steady flow, holding my legs into my chest. Resting my forehead between my knees, I started crying with sorrow and frustration as the tears and water fell from my face.

For the first time since Ben had died, I told God I was sorry.

Following my apology, I also told him that was how I felt. I was being honest. I reminded him that he had signed up to carry my pain and anger.

> And now he was telling me to quit? What was I going to do if I couldn't rail at him all the time? Did this mean I was entering another level of acceptance?

From that day on, I stopped bitching at God so severely and let up on the alcohol a bit. I still drank every day, but not enough to make myself pass out. The medications were taboo. I didn't know what else to do at the time, so I took the prescribed amounts and kept everything in moderation as best I could.

Apparently that morning's compromise was all it took and we had an understanding. I knew God was up to something, but I wasn't ready to admit my interest in him. He was not off the hook yet, not by a long shot.

Chapter 11

Cabo Wabo Christmas

Someone who thinks death is the scariest thing doesn't know a thing about life.
                                                ~ *Sue Monk Kidd*

The Holidays. I had a new understanding and appreciation as to why the suicide rates soared during these six weeks. The grieving pains were magnified times a thousand through a period that's incredibly over-celebrated and insanely cheery. I was cracking under its weight.

Simple words or phrases like: happy, merry, good tidings, peace on earth, season's greetings, jolly, that used to bring the warm and fuzzies, now made me want to drop a bunch of acid and find the nearest bridge.

I had decided in November that I wanted to get the hell out of Dodge during Christmas. I couldn't stand being around my extended family or Ben's family or the homes that we had spent past Christmases. I wanted to go somewhere that didn't celebrate or recognize the holiday. When we realized that demand had severely limited our options down to desert plains or jungle country, I was willing to compromise.

Karen, our extrovert and family travel agent, set off immediately in planning the vacation, and chose Cabo San Lucas, Mexico. We were also big Van Halen fans and loved Sammy Hagar. He owned a cantina in Cabos, so they were all excited to see one of his performances. Josh, Dusty, and I had left the house at 4:00 am Christmas morning, and by 2:00 pm Pacific time, we crossed the border and landed in Los Cabos. My granddaughter Katie had wanted to spend Christmas day with her family, so Karen stayed home with her and they would fly in tomorrow.

On our drive over to the resort, I felt a knot forming in my stomach. Which, surprisingly, was not from fear of our vehicle erratically flying off the over-crowded, narrow street into our gruesome, certain peril caused by the driver's terrifying driving skills, or severe lack of them.

Everywhere I looked there were Christmas decorations adorning the streets, stores, and of course, our resort. My goal had been to get as far away from this holiday shit as possible and I was furious that it had followed me all the way to Mexico.

We checked in at our resort and its stunning beauty momentarily soothed my frustration. The lobby was spacious and had bright, shiny embellished floors, verdant palm trees, and no walls or windows, just warm sunrays and tropical sea breezes drifting through to greet us.

We each had our own rooms and after unpacking, my sons and I headed out to see the sights. Beyond the impressive infinity pool, dotted with exotic plants and elegant cabanas, sat the dazzling Sea of Cortez, hugging the rough shoreline for miles with crystal clear blue water.

I tried soaking in the grandeur of it all, but my mind was far away. I had been tracking the day by remembering exactly what Ben I were doing one year ago, our last Christmas together, at that hour, and the next hour, and so on. I had never missed a family Christmas in my entire life and wondered now that I was here, in this serene, blissful escape from the ordinary, if I had made a huge mistake because I couldn't make the hurting stop.

> Was I trying to outrun my pain? Wasn't there anywhere I could go on this earth that grief wouldn't find me?

Scanning the endless expanse of sky and sea from the balcony, I was deep in thought when several knocks sounded from the front door. I squinted through the peephole and saw my sons. I had barely unlocked and opened the door for them to come in as Dusty asked non-rhetorically, "You ready to eat?"

"Yep," I said while grabbing my purse and room key, "Let's go."

They were ravenous after the long trip and wanted to find a local restaurant quickly, so I trailed behind listlessly, not too concerned about hunger or food. I happily settled for a few margaritas instead.

The next several days were pleasant enough. Karen and Katie flew in and made it to the resort safely the day after we had arrived. We hung out by the pool and stayed drunk most of the time. Although, we decided to drink in shifts for Katie, our twelve-year-old family member. We needed to at least *appear* like responsible adults.

By Wednesday we were ready for some activity and Karen had two options prepared for us: a dinner cruise or whale watching tour. When I saw that we would be going out to sea looking for whales in a yellow rubber raft, I looked up at my family and protested, "Oh no, hell no!"

If we were heading into the deep sea looking for massive mammals, I was not traveling in a dinky raft. "If y'all really want to do this, I want a boat." They looked back at me exasperated.

We stepped aboard the dinner cruise boat, spotted a booth cornering the bow, claimed our spot, and left port shortly after. Dinner was served buffet style on the main deck, but I didn't eat. Food was still unappealing to me and I mainly stuck to drinking.

We toured around several ports and spectacular coves and soon found ourselves approaching a whale-watching group. Our captain asked his crew if we wanted to follow the raft, and everybody answered yes.

The sun was slowly setting while we surveyed the deep blue waters excitedly for a dorsal fin or blowhole spray from below. Then, as if they had deliberately hid underwater until the perfect moment, a pod of orcas surfaced. While they swam along, the blood-orange sun gently kissed the vast horizon, melting away into the shimmering sea behind them. A palpable hush of reverential silence settled over the group as we watched nature showing off its magnificence and that experience became the highlight of our trip.

The day before New Year's Eve, Sammy Hagar was playing at his cantina, and when we arrived, the mood was laid back and happy. Sammy came out to perform with a few other musicians while we ate dinner and washed down several drinks, but I was pacing myself tonight.

Later on, after we strolled through the city shops, I laid awake in bed with my granddaughter fast asleep next to me. I couldn't shut off my mind as it plummeted me into heavy despair.

At 2:00 am, I quickly changed out of my pajamas, grabbed my sandals and the room key, and took the elevator down to the lobby. I was startled to see the resort was still bustling in the wee hours of the morning. Everything was so bright and people were working around the lobby, cleaning the pool and lounge areas, and carrying on as though it was the middle of a workday.

After walking down dozens of steps, I stopped and sat down on the last step next to a retaining wall, and faced the empty shore. I began minimizing my situation and my pain, feeling increasingly smaller as I questioned myself to pieces.

> There were so many worse things that could happen in life. Was my husband's homicide such a big deal? Did anyone really care if there's one more widow, or one less person in the world? I knew I needed to *own* what had happened to me and give it weight. But why wasn't I handling my loss better? Why was I so self-consumed? I should be thinking about my kids, Karen, and Katie. Where's my faith? How could I have faith in something I doubted truly existed?

Soon the self-hatred kicked in and propelled me off the step and onto the darkened beach. I started walking towards the famous arches with the moonshine glowing over them, railing at myself and then at God. When I neared the water's edge, I realized I could cross this sea, but Ben wouldn't be waiting for me on the other side. I could go anywhere on planet earth and would never ever find him. However, I did know the one place he was waiting for me, and I knew just how to get there.

Slipping off my sandals and carefully setting the room key on top of them, I walked past the shoreline and stepped into the murky water. I felt the rough ocean floor pricking my feet, trying to dissuade my mission, but I kept wading out further. The blackness of night and sea were reflections of my despondent heart as it seeped into the core of my being.

I was living in the past with Ben, trying to survive the present while fearing the future. There was no light, no hope, no signs of life after death. I didn't have an ounce of peace or happiness in anything and I wanted it to end. God, in all of his wonderful, mighty wisdom and omniscience, wasn't throwing me a lifeline, or at least some indication that he cared. If he did decide to intervene, it was just enough to temporarily control the bleeding, but not enough to stop it. I was hemorrhaging and he wouldn't let me die.

I had dared God, begging him to *please* kill me countless times. I knew the alcohol and pills weren't working anymore. Inebriation was great at taking the edge off, like a local anesthetic that numbs the surface area, but nothing could reach or go as deep as my pain. I was a dead woman walking anyway.

> How could mind-altering substances work on something that had no life? Suicide was my only option; my ultimate coping mechanism and final "fuck you" at God since he wouldn't do the honors himself.

The ocean water was cold and calm. I wasn't scared or even aware of sea urchins or other life-threatening animals lurking just below the surface. I had one goal on the mind: *Keep walking out until I couldn't touch the bottom, don't swim, and open my mouth.*

There were no tears, no fear or sadness, just rage. God was on trial tonight. I was the judge and he was guilty. My hatred and yelling intensified the deeper I waded. I didn't notice the water level quickly rising past my waist.

"You think I have to live this way, I'm not!" I screamed at him. "You think you have control over everything?! Well not anymore. I'll show you who's in control." I was going to see Ben and be with him forever, and I wouldn't hurt anymore. This was it, my one-way ticket out of this hell, and I would finally be free. Nothing could stop me as I felt the lulling waves envelop my body.

"I'll let you do this," God quietly interrupted.

What?! I snapped, pausing briefly with the water hovering around my shoulders. I peered into the endless void as if I would see his glowing form standing somewhere out there.

"You can do this. You will be with me and I will let you do this," he explained patiently, "But what about the boys?"

Instantly, the scene played out in front of me. Instead of seeing night, dark water, dark sky, I saw daylight and my sons. They were panic-stricken, frantically running all over the resort the next morning. "Mom, mom, mom!" They screamed in terror, "Where are you?!"

In a flash, I saw Josh and Dusty and the incredible fear on their faces, and it broke me. I felt my suicide mission derailing. I couldn't find the will to keep moving forward into the sea.

"I can't do that to them," I cried back, shaking my head sadly. I couldn't bear the thought of them losing their mom *and* dad in the same year. "They've been through too much! I can't. I can't."

"Good," he said. "Now get your ass back on the beach and deal with it."

I turned around slowly, thinking his tone seemed a little harsh, but I obeyed anyway and walked back to the shoreline. I sat down on the sand hugging my knees into my chest and started sobbing heavily. I was mad at myself for not going through with the plan, knowing I would never get that close to doing it again. Now I had no choice but to live the way I was living, *just trying to breathe.*

But why? For what? What kind of life *is that?*

"I don't know what you expect of me!" I wept loudly. "You put this person in my life and we loved each other!" That was us, our life. Ben and I had lived and loved. Love poured in and out, in and out, like the tide rolling in front of me.

And now it's gone? Where did it go; was it dammed up somewhere in the great unknown?

"What am I supposed to do with this love for him?" I shouted between tears, purely frustrated, not expecting an answer.

"You will love and be loved again," he comforted softly.

I let his words settle into my wandering soul and gazed into the nothingness. After a few quiet minutes, feeling completely exhausted, I treaded up the beach, through the pool area, and back into civilization. I noticed people staring at me as I walked through the lobby with puffy red eyes and sopping wet clothes clinging to my body, but I didn't care.

All I could think about was that I came out of the water and didn't drown myself. I hadn't experienced any miraculous healing, revelation, peace, or renewed faith, just another bout of depressing results: *the pain remained and I felt exactly the same.*

Opening and closing the room door as quietly as possible, I tiptoed past the bed, making sure Katie was still asleep, and went into the bathroom where I collapsed in defeat onto the cold marble floor. The secret weapon I was holding against God had been exposed and taken from me without a fight. I had found a small but comforting pleasure in the illusion that I could manipulate God, or pay him back by committing suicide, and now it was dispelled in one fell swoop.

Vowing to never tell a soul what I had just done, or attempted to do, I stripped off my damp t-shirt, shorts, and sports bra, threw them in the corner, and covered the clothes with dirty bath towels. I put my pajamas back on and dejectedly crawled into bed.

On New Year's Eve, the resort threw a big fiesta with an immaculate buffet dinner serenaded by a mariachi band, and fireworks on the beach at midnight. Tonight was the only time I could remember actually sitting down for a meal and consuming food.

When one of the servers came to our table holding a large tequila bottle, I automatically tilted my head back with my mouth wide open as he free poured a shot through the spout. He came by our table several times and I was ready and waiting for each round.

We spent most of New Year's day sleeping off our hangovers by the pool, and then packing for the trip home. I purposefully left the clothes I wore into the ocean where I had hidden them. I didn't want to bring home any reminders of that night.

By early evening of the next day, I walked through the front door of my house with no one to welcome me home, no happiness to be home, only the dread of facing the week ahead.

I threw my luggage into the bedroom, sprawled out on the sofa and lived there for the next six days in waiting. Not knowing what to expect when the actual day came, I laid around sad and scared.

> Was it going to be terribly painful realizing a year had gone by already without Ben? Or was it going to be a happy day, commemorating Ben, and being thankful that I had survived a whole year without him?

When January the eighth arrived, the latter option won; I was miserable. My cell phone was ringing non-stop but I didn't want to talk to anyone. I wanted to be left alone to hide from the world.

My faithful sister drove me over to the cemetery, but I hated visiting his grave. I didn't sense Ben's or God's presence there, and it had not been a place where I came to grieve. There was no life, just an empty space of stone, fake flowers, a pond, and piles of poop left behind from the migrant geese.

After our outing, Joan dropped me off at home, and like always, I went straight to the freezer for the Grey Goose, camped out on the sofa with my bottle and shot glass, and watched T.V. for the evening until I couldn't hold my eyes open.

Cabo Wabo Christmas

Chapter 12

The Veil

Mine was a patchwork God, sewn together from bits of rag and ribbon, Eastern and Western, pagan and Hebrew, everything but the kitchen sink and Jesus.
~ *Anne Lamott*

Another spring had passed, another season representing change and new life. I had survived the one-year mark, but I could no longer say or think, "A year ago Ben and I were doing this or that." I had entered a new unknown, I was accepting my loss.

During one of my sessions at Simply Grace, the Director, Ken, had asked if I was ready to start thinking about dating. I gave him a fast and hard no.

What is it with people trying to fix me up with men? Who are they to decide if and when I'm out of mourning?

Like I was in any shape to be in a relationship anyway. I was not about to throw myself into the dating scene, hoping to land Mr. Right, only to be miserably disappointed in discovering that he wasn't Ben. I had watched others cope by attaching their grief and neediness to a new partner. The relationship never lasted long and was doomed from the get go. I didn't want to suck the life from someone just to meet my own needs. I wasn't ready.

Ken hadn't finished with our session and wasn't letting my knee-jerk response deter what he wanted to say. "You *can* think about it Bekki. You're not married anymore," he said gently.

"No, I can't!" I had fought back, but I knew better.

I had run out of coping methods for self-protection and now I couldn't avoid the obvious. Somehow I was supposed to move out of my preferable seclusion. My friend-turned-counselor's uncomfortably honest words had dropkicked me into the acceptance phase of my grieving. With this new recognition came reality, and with reality came bitterness.

The reality that I wasn't married to Ben anymore was extremely painful and difficult to receive. Even though I had arrived at this stage, it didn't mean I was fixed. I tried convincing myself that because I had made it one year, the worst was behind me. I could re-invent myself and become my own woman, a better version of me.

However, when nothing felt better and there weren't any noticeable changes in me, I steadily fell into despair. I had a lot of things going absolutely nowhere and couldn't find steady ground to make a few steps forward in life. I was tired of feeling like a nameless nomad, wandering through a wasteland I hadn't volunteered to enter; I was blindfolded and led. And God still wasn't helping or intervening with any shimmering nuggets of truth and renewal.

I tore through self-help books and literature about grief and healing, desperately searching for a new angle or different approach to feel better. I was running from what I knew I needed to do: sit, just sit in the terrible pain.

I had tried Reiki sessions several times. A Reiki practitioner found one of my chakras had been clogged because of trauma, but that wasn't anything I didn't already know, so I kept searching. I had scheduled an appointment with a Reunionist to go through my lineage for some reunion therapy. She had come into my home, zeroing in on my Native American ancestry because she was tuned into their culture and spirit world. But Reunionism didn't do much for me either and I didn't invite her back.

The only people that kept my attention and that I felt drawn to were psychics. The first time I had visited one was last September. My adventurous friend DeeAnn agreed to accompany me because I was a bit nervous, but excited too.

I had told her I wanted to see one in the next town just to avoid bumping into anyone I knew from our neck of the woods. She sighed exasperatedly and rolled her eyes, but had followed through with my request and found us a psychic.

We pulled into the parking lot of a small shopping center where the new age storefront was located and drove around to the back entrance. Being a novice psychic goer that I was, I had figured this was a back-door type of deal and was trying to be covert.

I knocked on the metal door and waited impatiently for someone to greet us, but no one ever came. I knocked again with more force and listened for a voice, footsteps, something. Still no answer. Then DeeAnn looked at me with a silly grin. "Shouldn't they know we're here?" She laughed. "Aren't they supposed to be psychics?"

I chuckled quietly, but really just wanted to get inside the store before we were noticed. It had taken us a few more seconds to realize we were, in fact, at the wrong door as we drove back to the front side of the building and found the main entrance.

We walked in and saw crystals and rocks, gargoyles, jewelry, and new age books lining the walls. The atmosphere felt very peaceful and quiet, similar to a day spa with gentle, soothing music drifting through the air.

The receptionist greeted us calmly and escorted us back into one of the private rooms for our readings. Maybe I had expected elaborate curtains, sheers draping the ceiling and walls, a crystal ball or two, some incense burning; anything more gypsy-like.

But this was just a cozy little room with three folding chairs, a card table with a green tablecloth, a babbling water fountain, and a dimly lit floor lamp for extra ambiance.

The psychic came in and we took turns introducing ourselves. I had decided beforehand that I wouldn't give her any information about me or lead her in any way. If she was a psychic, she could tell me, she was supposed to know anyway, and I wanted to get my money's worth.

I liked the woman already and was impressed at how secure she was in herself. She was dressed in business attire and conducted herself professionally, not fruit-loopy or some strung-out mystic; she was very peaceful and reassuringly present.

I wanted to go first, and when we sat down, she asked to see my right hand. I had learned that whichever hand was dominant, that one carried my present and future, and the other carried my past. She gently held my hand, tracing the lines with her fingers, and explained what each line meant. When she saw my emotional and relational lines, she stopped and looked up at me.

"You lost someone very close to you," she said softly. "He died tragically, very suddenly."

Immediately the tears welled up in my eyes and I started crying, but staying resolute, I didn't confirm or deny what she was reading. She said those two lines came to a very abrupt stop and that was how she knew I had experienced a terrible loss.

"He's okay," she comforted, "He crossed over and is on the other side. His spirit is here with me now." At that point, I began freak-ing out inside and tried to maintain composure while she casually continued.

"You have two boys. They will be fine. There's a dark haired little girl. You are very important in her life." She was talking about my granddaughter Katie. "You have to keep going for her."

She looked at me again and said, "You're going to be okay. You *will* survive this."

I sat very still, listening intently while the psychic read a few more things, and then she picked up her stack of tarot cards. Divvying them out on the table in three stacks of thirteen cards, she then asked me to pick one stack. I had chosen the middle pile and she turned them over, forming a cross with the cards. The card in the middle was my main reading, and when she told me what card it was, I was amazed.

I looked down and saw an older woman dressed in black with a black cloak covering her head and she was sadly staring out the window. The card represented my widowhood. Then a lawyer card came up, which was a man dressed in a suit, standing inside a court room with books stacked up beside him, and she said I had a lot of legal issues happening right now. I could not believe how dead on she was as she had proceeded in explaining the other cards. From that time on, whenever I went in for an appointment, she read my mail.

I tried seeing different psychics with the same skeptical attitude, but they nailed my life *every* time. The exact same cards would turn up, even after I had made sure to choose a different stack from a previous visit.

The psychics gave me peace, more peace than I had ever felt reading through dozens of books about heaven, death and the after-life of our spirit, or healing from loss. They knew my life and after they finished my readings, each psychic always comforted and encouraged me, saying I would to get through this, I would be okay, and the season would pass.

I had never sensed anything evil or demonic. I was never afraid when I was with them. I would tell them I was a Christian and believed in Jesus. Most would say they did too and prophesying was one of their giftings of the Spirit.

I was intrigued by how easily they accepted death, that it was a passing or crossing over, and not a finality to them. The veil was so thin between this life and the next, and to them, it was just like breathing. The psychics were in tune with the spirit life and spirit world. I was compelled to go back because it had become a lifeline to Ben, a reassuring connection to him, and a pleasant distraction. I became hooked and fascinated by the paranormal. Although, deep down, I knew it was just another form of control, another middle finger at God, another way to cope.

I wanted answers; someone to tell me what was coming around the corner. After being blind-sided by a major life-altering loss, I was still reeling, trying to put my life back together. I felt ill equipped, like I couldn't make the pieces fit, or worse yet, I didn't have any pieces. I had no leads or hints, no instruction manual or deific words of wisdom on where to start or how to ever begin again. The one clue I had in my possession was protected and kept hidden from sight.

Nine years ago, I had been part of an intercessory prayer team with our church and attended the women's group weekly prayer meeting. During those sessions, we prayed together and would then go into separate rooms and pray individually.

One day, I was talking to God by myself, and he said I would be widowed young, and I instantly began weeping. I told God that his prophecy was the saddest thing he had ever told me and his words frightened me.

When I showed the head intercessor, she didn't know what to do or say. She instructed me to write down whatever God had said to me. Later that week I had decided to show Ken and DeeAnn. They didn't know how to respond either, and ever since then, I had forgotten what God told me.

Three weeks after Ben's death, I remembered what I had written. I found the torn page tucked away in one of my journals and read it again. I started crying and became mad at myself. I didn't understand why God would tell me such a horrible truth *nine years* before Ben died. But if God had allowed me to remember, would I have tried to control Ben's life with the knowledge that he could die any day? Every time I went to the psychics, they always told me I was very intuitive and just needed to pay attention.

> Then why didn't I say anything when Ben brought the motorcycle home that day? Why did I ever let him buy the stupid thing in the first place? How could I have forgotten that I was going to be widowed young?

Even though the prophecy pissed me off and began a whole new line of questioning with God, I felt comforted in a way. Now I found solace in the fact that he was letting me know he was in control. Ben's death wasn't just something awful that happened, and somehow it was part of God's messed up plans.

Chapter 13

F*** the Neighbors

Pain narrows vision. The most private of sensations, it forces us to think of ourselves and little else.
  ~ *Phillip Yancey*

The dog days of summer were in full effect, forcing everyone into premature hibernation to wait out the long, hot and sticky days, or else find some reprieve by the water. My family had always spent the summers in the pool either at Joan and Doug's house or Ben's and mine old house.

During the past few months, I had been constantly invited to get out of the house and go swimming, but it was still too hard. Ben and I spent a lot of time and had many fond memories at the poolside. I wasn't ready to revisit them. However, I had gradually started going out in public and spent more time with my family and at Simply Grace. I was growing accustomed to living alone, cooking for one, balancing checkbooks, and other chores I had once taken for granted.

The lawsuit had continued unfolding and our case was growing stronger. I still didn't know much of what was happening on the forefront, but I knew we were doing well. The legalities of it all, the lawyers, investigators, analysts, affidavits, and depositions felt intimidating to me, so I chose to remain detached until I was needed.

I noticed that I was beginning to have some consistent gray days, which had been an encouraging step and relieving break from the depressingly black days, weeks, and months that had once loomed heavily over my heart. I was starting to catch my breath.

The feelings of brokenness and sadness remained my constant companions. I had not let God off the hook yet. We were still at war. Although, the painful sharp reminders that Ben was gone and I was alone forever had subsided, mostly during the sober hours, into a constant dull throb.

One afternoon, I had been sitting by my bedroom window, watching the birds, not thinking about anything in particular, when God decided to stop by for an unplanned visit. Before Ben's death, I had welcomed these moments with God. I sought out the quiet times and was eager to sit and be with him. But now, I despised that stillness and ran from it. I wasn't fond of his surprises anymore, not after the worst bombshell of my life.

I liked believing I had control of our time together, or that I dictated when and how he could talk to me, like he had to ask for my permission first. But I was learning that he was a little crazy. He did whatever he wanted to do anyway, whenever he wanted to do it.

That afternoon he had showed me a mother leaning over a dressing table, tenderly caring for her newborn child. She was so delicate and loving with her fragile infant, as if it was the most precious thing in the world to her. I could feel the love of this mother, the vulnerability and great dependency of the baby.

Then he said that was how he had been caring for me. He *knew* my pain, he was with me *in* and *through* it, but I was hurting too much to notice him. All I could see, think, or feel was my grief and mourning, rage and bitterness, and I had no awareness of him. But he was waiting for me.

He knew what I needed and gave me space to grieve, even though I hated him for being distant most of the time. I was still trying to figure him out, or understand why he would allow me to experience such a painful loss not just in my life, but my family's as well.

I tried getting along with him or at least remain on speaking terms, but my feeble attempts usually lasted a few hours, or maybe a workday. *Somehow it was just easier to stay mad at him.*

I continued struggling in the evenings, at bed time, weekends, and especially Sunday afternoons, because that was when Ben and I had our time alone and were most intimate. I would drink my way through those hours and stayed on my prescriptions, even though I had begun questioning whether I really needed the pills anymore, and one day I had found the answer.

Knowing a visit was long over-due; I needed to see my mother. Before leaving my house after lunch, I hesitated briefly, checking myself to see if I had enough strength to mentally prepare for such a visit. I had determined I could handle her.

I didn't look forward to the mom visits, and actually, I dreaded seeing her. She was an eight-two-year-old widow who stayed tweaked out on pills and was bitter at the world. Every time I came over, she would incessantly whine, moan, and groan that she was suffering from her newest, self-diagnosed ailment. My mom was delusional and it drove me up the wall. I had wondered when God took Ben, why hadn't he taken this woman, who was incredibly miserable and hated her life, at the same time?

"You took this man who was full of life, living life, working hard and having a damn good time doing it all, and you leave her?" I challenged him. She was so bitter and nobody could do anything to please her.

How was I supposed to comfort her when I was desperately questing for my own? Was I co-depending her? Was I letting the expectations of others get in my head?

I had turned onto my mom's street, and as I drove through the quaint and quiet neighborhood, I took a few conscious breaths, reassuring myself I would be okay. My other sister Faye greeted me when I walked in and immediately warned me that mom was already off and running on one of her tangents. Today, she had cancer.

I braced myself and found mom sitting, as always, in her beige recliner and staring out the back window. I hated this house because she loved keeping everything dark, dreary, and depressing. At times, I could almost see her resemblance to the Gollum creature from Lord of the Rings, just wasting away all alone in her cave, obsessed with her precious little life.

I was about to sit down with her when my cellphone rang. Hiding my relief that the call had spared me a few minutes away, I went into the garage to talk. When I came back, I caught the ending to one of her multiple griping sessions, and apparently, that was the last straw.

"Why don't you just *die*?! Why do you want to live, just die already!" I shouted furiously and threw my phone at her. "You wanna die... go ahead. Why are you afraid you have cancer? Big deal! You'll die and get to be with dad and Ben and Jesus!"

I was enraged, but she seemed oblivious to everything I had just yelled in her face. She nonchalantly looked over at my sister Faye and plainly said, "Well, I certainly hope the *neighbors* aren't hearing this."

Glaring at her insidiously, I couldn't believe even in her warped, strung out, state-of-mind, she still had enough pride to care about what others might think or say. I had grown up with those irritating, selfish remarks to always "be mindful of the neighbors" ringing in my ears. Now it felt like nails scraping against the chalkboard and I was done.

I politely stomped past her to the front door, unlocked half a dozen bolts and chains, and flung the heavy wooden door back at the wall. Kicking the storm door out in front of me, I angrily stepped onto the front porch, took in a deep breath, and screamed at the top of my lungs, "Fuuuuuuuck the neighbors!"

Listening to my words echo down the street, I felt satisfied with my release and casually walked back into the living room. As if the juvenile episode had been perfectly warranted, I held my head high and met my sister's chastising glare.

"I think you need to go home now," She said evenly.

Not letting her tone or looks faze me, I cordially replied, "Yes. I think I do."

I left my mother's house and spent the night mulling over my episode. I was afraid. I scared myself at how quickly I had jumped in the other ditch. I had never acted out that way in my entire life, and I knew this was *not* healthy. I felt the bitterness haunting me and I didn't want it to get too comfortable.

The hardest thing to realize from my reaction was I saw myself in my mom. She was there, she had been stuck there for years, festering in unforgiveness, and it had infected her own well-being. I was heading down that road too, faster than I wanted to admit. Something needed to change.

Better, not bitter, remember? I told myself.

When I woke up this morning, I called my doctor right away. I had a huge fear of coming off the prescriptions.

> What if I had another meltdown or what if I couldn't cope with the pain? Was I truly healing, or was it the meds kicking in? Was that you God, or was that my happy pills?

I was scared of revisiting that dark place, but the desire for change trumped my fears. I was sick and tired of questioning the better days. I had an ideal or principle if I lived through my grieving, I wanted to come out on the other side proclaiming God was the only thing that helped me, but that fantasy had died a long time ago. Then I wondered if I was ashamed of myself for giving in or being weak, that I wasn't the strong woman of faith I thought I had been, even though my life had been shattered and drastically changed forever.

> Was it religion creeping in, shaming me into my old beliefs that I needed to "keep up appearances"? Did I have to accept what life had dealt me, or what God had given me with no ifs, ands, or buts about it?

I let the pondering swirl around in my head as I waited on hold, and ironically heard the voice recording colorfully advertise the benefits of taking my prescription. While I listened to the extensive hazards of the particular pills, I couldn't help but laugh at how the list of possible side effects sounded worse than the initial problem being treated.

When the doctor answered the phone, I told him what had happened yesterday. I firmly said I did not want to be out-of-control anymore. *I didn't want the medications controlling me* and I was ready to quit. The doctor listened empathetically and consented to lower my dosage. He gave me specific instructions on how to wean off of them and finally be done forever. I was a little disappointed in hearing that the process couldn't happen over night, but I was willing to start anywhere, whatever it took.

Chapter 14

12 Doughnuts & A Switchblade

The opposite of love is not hate, it's indifference... The opposite of faith is not heresy, it's indifference. The opposite of life is not death, it's indifference.

~ Elie Wiesel

The second anniversary of Ben's death had arrived and, unlike the year before, I didn't go out of the house or talk to anyone besides my family. The day had passed slowly and uneventfully, filling the hours and my heart with the ever-constant oppressive sadness.

Coming off the prescriptions was going well so far, and fortunately my fears did not manifest; I hadn't experienced any more breakdowns or anxiety attacks. I slowly started counseling again after reviewing the fine print of my terms and conditions with Ken. I would not be Simply Grace's poster child for grief. I was not ready to counsel widows, or anyone for that matter, who were struggling with their grieving process. He agreed and carefully chose which counselees to send my way. I also began co-leading our night group, because up until this class, I had only sat in and listened.

The summer meltdown had been a wake-up call. I needed to stop hiding and isolating and engage with life and the community. I had started attending church with Karen, but not without difficulty.

I hated how alone I felt. Even in the midst of thousands of people, I felt like the loneliest person in the world, as if the masses surrounding me merely heightened the aloneness. I was still only half of a whole.

I had recently completed my first successful trip to the local grocery store without morphing into a puddled, teary mess at the sight of Ben's preferred peanut butter on the shelf. I was never fond of grocery shopping anyway, but after Ben died, that errand had been extremely challenging. Usually I would vacate my half-full cart in the middle of whichever aisle had triggered the pain and ran out of the store sobbing. All of my husband's name-brand items I used to buy special for him were now banned from my grocery list.

A second holiday season had come and gone and I did not try and run away. I stood in front of the swelling waves of grief and let them pound into me. Yes, there were many painful moments and memories, but I had been able to sit through the pain and I survived.

We had celebrated Christmas the traditional way. Josh, Karen, Katie, and Dusty came over to my house on Christmas Eve and Karen taught me how to shag to the tunes of Marvin Gay. Christmas Day was spent at mom's house with the extended family. I had refused to cook or bake any of Ben's favorite dishes and everybody was okay with my decision.

I had brought in the New Year by staying with Joan and Doug at their mountain house. The college football games were streaming constantly and the family had been on each other's last nerve. I was sad during my stay, but glad to be away from home. Ben and I had loved to watch the snowfall because it was a rare treat in the South. We were like little kids, giddy with excitement whenever snow had come to spread its glistening white blanket over the tired ground.

Thankfully the weather cooperated with my moodiness and held back the snow showers until I left.

Today I was not so lucky. Gray clouds darkened the sky, emptying out cold and heavy rains that somehow crept into my soul. Valentine's Day was a week away and I caught myself wishing I had something to celebrate as I sat by my window with the phone at arm's reach.

Earlier in the day, one of my friends had called and asked if I was willing to talk to his friend who was in trouble. He had stayed on the phone with her the entire night, trying to calm her down, and then figured I could be more helpful. I had told him that was fine, but I started feeling angry the more I thought about his request.

> Who did he think I was? Just because I was suffering, did that qualify me to talk someone else of the ledge? I didn't have any answers for this person. I didn't have answers for myself.

Finally, after nearly ten hours had passed of waiting for her call and stewing in my own self-loathing, my cell phone lit up and I answered cordially. Wading through all the introductory formalities, I listened attentively to see if she would open up or if I needed to prompt her. My impatience won and I jumped in first.

"So…what's goin' on?" I asked carefully.

There was a slight pause and then a labored sigh, "Well, my life is in the crapper," she blurted out. "I'm going through a really hard time right now…and I'm tired of living." She said, as her voice quivered heavily. She went on to explain what had happened that led her to this bleak disposition in life. Then we both sat in sober contemplation as she cried quietly and occasionally sniffled.

"And, I would've called you sooner," she said breaking the long silence, "but I had to run an errand down to the specialty bakery shop and order a dozen gourmet doughnuts."

What? I thought curiously. "What are you talking about 'a special order of gourmet doughnuts'?"

"*You know*, they make 'em to order," she said, as if everyone in the world knew about these specialty doughnut shops.

I was almost amused at what I was hearing while she proceeded to elaborately detail the variety of flavors, frosting, and toppings she had ordered. I managed to suppress my sick-humored tendencies for her sake, and responded in my trained, professional mannerism, "Well, do you have a plan?"

"Yah," she answered casually, "I'm sitting here, talking to you, and I have a switchblade at my wrist right now. I want to end my life."

Before censoring the gravity of my reply, I flippantly said, "Go ahead. Do it. God'll let you. But every woman will hate you if you kill yourself with a dozen, fresh, gourmet doughnuts on the table."

I was playing with fire but didn't care because I had been there. I wanted to call her bluff and find out if she actually had the nerve to execute her plan. Then, a startling burst of weepy laughter resounded from the other end; she thought I was joking. I cracked a smile, glad she could handle some sarcasm, but I was still serious.

I told her my story and that I understood where she was at, how she was feeling, and that she could kill herself, but she would leave a lot of pain and heartache behind. She was looking for a way out. She was in the middle of her doctorate degree but couldn't seem to finish. Her roommate and best friend had just moved away and now she lived alone in a dirty apartment because she was too depressed to clean, and to top it off, she was in severe debt.

Without thinking twice about offering a bed in my house to a complete stranger, I invited her to come down for a week to stay with me and attend our Simply Grace classes. She wasn't jumping up and down with the idea, just moments after threatening suicide, and said she needed time to think it over and would call me later with her decision.

As soon as we hung up, I felt my mind and emotions plunging south. I had taken on her sadness. This was exactly why I wasn't ready to counsel the heavy cases. I couldn't handle another's issues because mine were still too fresh.

Tossing my previous resolutions out the window, I instinctively walked straight to the kitchen cabinet, grabbed my favorite shot glass and pulled out a fresh bottle of Grey Goose from the freezer. I parked my dilapidated ass in front of the fireplace and kept pouring until the pain stopped and had drunk myself to sleep.

Sometime later, a warm, wet something was tickling my feet and wouldn't quit. Trying to awake from my drunken stupor, I slowly raised my head just enough to see my dog patiently asking to go outside. My head immediately started swimming and I had to drop back down onto the pillows.

Why are my feet exposed if I'm in bed and under the covers? I thought. I knew it was still dark out but there was enough light coming from the fireplace to see the dog. *What am I doing on the living room floor?*

I looked up again and saw a red quilt wrapped tightly around my body and I was completely naked. Wondering how I had taken off my clothes and wrapped myself in a blanket on the floor was beyond my intoxicated ability to figure out. I stood up carefully, still cuddled inside my quilted cocoon, and let the dog out to pee.

After turning off the fireplace, I waddled through the dark into my room and landed on the bed with a disgruntled sigh.

> Would I ever be healthy enough to not let myself get sucked in with other's grief and misery? Would there be a day when I didn't have to use alcohol to cope? I thought I had been doing better. What do the nights like tonight mean? Why did I feel so lost again?

I realized where the questioning was heading and stopped before I felt any worse about myself and, letting my brain relax, I fell back to sleep.

Chapter 15

Peace Treaty

Why does our trust offer such immense pleasure to God? Because trust is the preeminent expression of love.
~ Brennan Manning

I sat in my car with the engine still running, gazing blankly at the dashboard clock. *3:02 pm. What the hell am I doing here?* Of all the places I wanted to avoid, somehow I had ended up at the epicenter.

Each of my family members had special plans prepared for the day with their spouses. Not wanting to intrude on anyone's celebrating or be the third wheel, I decided to get gussied up and head into town. Actually, I was trying to endure Valentine's Day. The whole week leading up to today had put me in a depressed funk of feeling cheated and angry, but self-medicating was not an option this year.

For the third time around, I had resigned with the reality that days like these would not get easier unless I chose to face them head-on. The decision to sit through whatever grievous tides swept over me and wait it out had seemed healthy a week ago; however, it had proved to be no easy feat.

I had grimaced my way through T.V. shows as every other commercial flaunted an inspiring floral arrangement, romantic card, or dazzling jewelry piece that perfectly captures and articulates a man's undying love and affection. The commercial continued as the woman breathlessly accepts his heart-winning gift in complete and utter scripted surprise. Whimsically throwing her arms around his neck and showering him with adoring smiles, the woman would finish the moment with a dreamy, tender kiss.

I would then suppress the raging impulse to dismember the television and hurl it through the bedroom window, while cursing the wretched day, vowing to never celebrate love and romance ever again.

I awoke this morning with heavy sadness, which had been expected, and I had a survival plan. I would pace myself in preparing for the day and, after showering, putting on some make-up, fixing my hair and dressing above my emotional status, I'd go out driving for the afternoon. I didn't have a specific destination in mind, so it was baffling to me that I had instinctively, more like subconsciously, chosen the mall to kill some time, the very place where this lovey-dovey bullshit would be rubbed in my face.

The parking lot was jam-packed, but my persistent serpentine search was rewarded. I managed to score a spot close to the main entrance to my favorite department store. I took one last deep breath and opened the car door. Immediately, the chilled winter air stung my exposed skin and I quickly pulled the coat zipper closed up to my chin. When I entered the store, I couldn't help but notice how many men were bustling around in a frenzied pace, shopping for a last minute, merchandised endearment, and a disdainful scowl crept over my face.

Give 'em a break, I told myself. *You're just sad because they remind you of Ben. This was exactly what he used to do. Keep moving.*

I meandered through the first floor for a while, not intending to purchase anything, and headed towards the escalators to check out the home department when I stopped suddenly near the jewelry section. Never in my life had I bought a piece of jewelry for myself, but something compelled me to look around at the over-whelming variety of shiny adornments for no reason in particular. After sifting through a few counter displays, a diamond pendant peace sign lying inside the locked case caught my eye.

Peace...yah. I thought. *Sure I would love world peace.* Then, out of nowhere, a light bulb turned on. *What about making peace with God?*

Warm tears instantly sprung to my eyes at the thought. *Peace with God? What does that look like?* I knew I didn't want to war with him anymore, but I had no idea how peace could ever happen.

The sales associate must have noticed me standing in front of her counter, wandering why I hadn't blinked or moved as I gazed intensely through the glass, but I was frozen in a mind-meld of detached contemplation.

"Hi there," she greeted sunnily, "May I help you with anything?"

Forcing down the uncomfortably enormous crying lump that lodged itself in my throat, I regained a measure of composure and pointed to the mid-size pendant, "Yes. I would like to see that necklace please."

"Aha. These peace symbols are very popular right now." The associate informed as she unlocked the case and daintily handed the sparkling piece to me.

I held the pendant and examined it closely, calculating the cost because I was unsure about spending that much money on myself, but I knew I was supposed to buy it.

Okay God, I'm going to splurge for you, I said silently, *this is my Valentine's gift to you.* "It reminds me of my hippie days," I told her with a forced smile, and decided against revealing the true meaning of this purchase. "I'd like to buy it."

"Wonderful!" She beamed, "And will you be needing a chain to go with it?"

"Yah, I would."

I watched her sort through an assortment of lengths, colors, and styles of chains. She came back holding up a medium-length, diamond cut, white-gold chain and waited for my opinion. Approving of her choice, I bought both items and asked her to put the necklace on for me. She happily obliged.

Right then and there, with the beautiful new pendant resting on my chest, I was ready to surrender. Gently waving my white flag at God, I declared,

No more war.

We had made our peace treaty standing in the middle of a department store. I gave God my Valentine's Day gift, like a sucker. How I ended up here, doing the very thing I had spent the past week abominating, was undoubtedly, *a divine set-up.*

I had left feeling something vaguely familiar, but unrefined. It was so intangible and fragile; I was afraid if I named it, the feeling would shatter and evaporate as it had over three years ago. Like when the first flow of rainwater creeps into the parched, barren plains after a grueling dry season, bringing signs of new life in its wake. I had felt a small but distinct current of hope coursing through me.

Over the next several months, a restlessness began moving in me again. We were nearing the end of the Simply Grace class. I had channeled a lot of my energy and thought life into the group, and now I was sad in knowing it would soon be over. The woman I had more or less talked off the ledge, after playing a daring round of rush and roulette with God over a human life, accepted my offer to come and visit. She attended several Simply Grace classes and was hungry for more. Somehow my offer for a one-week stay in my home had eventually turned into an extended yearlong sabbatical from her other life.

I enjoyed having company, and her presence eased my loneliness. Granted our drunk hours may have outweighed the sober ones, but we got along well enough. We took turns processing each other's grief and our searching souls united us in a way. Unanswered questions still remained, making me feel fractured and incomplete. But instead of cursing and railing at God for his deliberate and irritating silence, I remembered my necklace, our special peace treaty. Enclosing my hand over the diamond pendant, I would hold it firmly against my chest until the rage had settled. One morning I was driving into work, mentally reviewing my schedule for the day, when God said, "You trust me."

"*Trust* you?! No. I do not trust you whatsoever." I sassed back, annoyed at how he liked to jump in and out, just to throw me off kilter.

"Yes, you do," he continued.

Really? Is he trying to get a rise out of me? I didn't respond, not wanting to encourage his little intrigue, hoping he would shut up and leave me alone; like that would stop him.

"You trust me enough to hate me."

I focused stubbornly on the road, trying to ignore his last comment, but it kept running through my head. He let me be after that, but I knew he would be back.

Why did he say that? Was he trying to prove a point or did he actually want to show me something?

A few weeks into April, we had bought tickets to see Bon Jovi perform in concert. I was genuinely excited, which was a pleasant surprise, to go out with the girls and see the man who put words to my pain, and had unknowingly walked with me through some desolate grieving periods.

As the concert was wrapping up, they performed their rendition of the Hallelujah song. I was mesmerized while I listened intently to the words. The truth of that song was impactful, and when I looked around the filled arena, all I could see were twenty thousand people raising their hands in the air and singing with him.

They were worshipping. At a Bon Jovi concert. It was a unified cry of worship to whatever god they believed in and hoped was listening. I was awestruck and swept away by the humbling beauty of surrender in that moment.

"You don't worship me like this anymore," God had said softly. I instantly burst into tears. He was right.

I know, I whispered back. *I know.*

He wasn't accusing me or saying it with expectation or demand for me to pick up the slack; he was just being honest with me. I wanted to forget the intimacy of worship. He knew what those special times had been between us and I chose to shut it down hard.

However, my cold shoulder was slowly turning back to him, my icy resignation towards anything spiritual had begun to thaw. He was still up to something and I wasn't resisting him. Instead of blaming God for taking away thirty-one years of a great marriage, I began feeling grateful for thirty-one amazing years he had given me with Ben.

I didn't want justification anymore; I desired restoration and healing. I let go of expecting God to "make the pain go away" and began trusting him with the process. I started seeing him in a different light, the God of *redemption*. I knew I could stay mad at him forever, and he would let me and love me just the same, but I was coming to the end of my anger. I wanted something more and was ready to drop my end of the rope.

Two months later I was ready to embark on a new journey. I had realized I didn't want Ben's death to define me anymore. I wanted to be more than his death. I knew I would have to get outside of my protected comfort zone at Simply Grace to find out what *life beyond death* looked like for me.

One day, I was chit-chatting with a former-student-turned-dear-friend, when she mentioned an Inner Healing class she had taken the year before. She said she would go through the class again with me if I wanted to step outside of my ministry. I had said I needed time to think it over and would let her know what I decided, but I already knew the answer. I called my friend back a couple days later and told her to put me on the list. When the day of the first class arrived, I wasn't exactly thrilled to start. I felt anxious and nervous about heading into another unknown and possibly having to feel more pain, but my desire for real change undermined the other emotions. I was ready to give up my anger.

The class was an intense ten weeks of looking through my past, facing the pain of certain experiences, and seeing the resulting lies and misbeliefs about God, myself, and others. I had to acknowledge the walls I had built high and wide for myself after Ben's death, the hatred and distrust I had with God, and the bondage that kept me distant in relationships.

Inner Healing class was like a total body, soul, and spirit boot camp on steroids. We were given homework assignments, chapters to read, and journal questions for God to answer, which was especially challenging. I gave up on going to him for guidance and hadn't journaled in at least six months.

Then there was the infamous stool. I had watched the other women go through their own "stool" time, and hoped that somehow I would be skipped or forgotten, but I had no such luck.

We were five weeks into the class and I was extremely worked up. The concept of forgiveness was irritating me and stirred up all of the anger, doubt, and hatred at God for Ben's death again. I was not going to run and hide this time and had resolved to sit and stew in my crap.

I used to challenge my counselees and students with my favorite question: *How* free *do you want to be?* Now, I was actually doing what I taught and learned it was much easier said than done. Freedom came at a price, a choice of the will. In order for something new to birth, I had to let go of the old. *But how?*

The teacher was exactly what I needed, someone to hold my feet to the fire. She could smell my stink a mile away and called me up to the front of the room. Feeling like I was back in elementary school with the entire class eyeing me, I obediently approached the stool, sat down, and closed my eyes.

After a few minutes of narrowing down the list of who I had left to forgive, it became obvious that God was the only one. As soon as his name was spoken, the emotional turmoil erupted.

"If you are my kinsman redeemer like you claim to be, then why would you let this happen to me? What kind of twisted freak are you? How could you? Why would you take him from me?!" I screamed, whipping my reading glasses at the floor. "Why don't you answer me? Haven't I done enough to deserve something, some response, *anything?!*"

The questions and accusations continued pouring out at him uncontrollably as the bitter rage shook my body. *Where is this coming from? Why am I feeling this again? I thought I made peace with him.*

My anger subsided and I opened my eyes to see if she had any further guidance. She said good job, patted me on the back, and dismissed me back to my chair.

Well, there it was, I let God have it again, in front of this class and that's it? So now what? I wondered, feeling incredibly disappointed.

I scooted up to the table with my book still open on the provoking forgiveness chapter. I looked at it, unable to read the words through my tearful fury, and suddenly the only thing I saw in blaring, emboldened letters was:

Forgive me.

What? I stopped instantly, recalling that those words hadn't been there a moment ago. I looked down again to double-check, in case my emotions had short-circuited a vital comprehension wire to my brain, but the two words were definitely written on the page, staring right back at me.

"Will you forgive me?" He asked.

I felt as though time was suspended and my soul had stumbled into present tense, where everything was quiet and still, and he and I were the only two beings in the universe.

You mean, me *forgive* you? I contested. *Why the hell would you ask me that? You don't need my forgiveness. Shouldn't I be pleading for your forgiveness? Isn't that blasphemous?"*

"Bekki. I'm asking you. Will you forgive me?" He persisted.

I just sat there, feeling like a first grader again, wide-eyed and ready to grasp such a profound concept, wanting the teacher's nod of approval for responding correctly. But my adult brain wasn't accepting the childlike impulse to just trust and jump.

Crickets.

I felt his question filling the air and surrounding me, not like the usual suffocating, claustrophobic way with grief, but in a warm, serene, and loving way.

I didn't know how to answer him. I knew what forgiveness was and was not. I had presented it numerous times and walked through the process myself, but I had never put God in the chair.

I didn't think he was an option.

Now I had to choose, he had left it up to me.

> Could I really let God off the hook? Was he *that* trusting to let me decide? To choose where our relationship would go from here? If I said yes, would we be buddy-buddy, frolicking through poppy fields and dancing into the sunset together?
>
> Would the pain go away forever?
>
> Would that mean I could never get mad at him, or be his submissive servant until I die because I "agreed"?
>
> What if I liked hating God? It was certainly easier than trying to get along.

I meticulously evaluated the risks to either answer, listing the pros and cons to a possible life-changing decision. I realized my list of debts against God would never be enough to satisfy my rage or fill the void.

Isn't this what I signed up for? Don't I want a change from my limited existence? I had tried everything else, which had always led to the same results, so I couldn't be any worse off than I was now. *Screw it.*

Yes, I flinched. *Yes, I forgive you God.*

Chapter 16

The Waiting Game

*God is ready to assume full responsibility for
the life wholly yielded to him.*
~ *Andrew Murray*

"Mrs. Dinsmore has made her decision," spoke my attorney. "She will not carry on with the wrongful death suit, and she has a few things she would like to say." He finished, gesturing for me to take the floor.

I observed the intimidating panel seated before me, dressed in formal business attire, looking at me less severely than a few moments ago, clearly relieved that the next several years of their lives wouldn't be spent with a lawsuit and jury trials hanging over their heads.

Josh, Dusty, the attorney, and I had just re-entered the mediation room after discussing our options concerning the case. Today we had to decide if we wanted to take the wrongful death suit to a Grand Jury, or settle with the air flight company's monetary offer.

When we had first arrived at the law office building and found the correct room, my sons, our attorney and I sat down at a large conference table. I was facing the owner of the company that had killed Ben, the owner's attorneys, and the mediator sitting just inches beyond my reach. My daughter-in-law Karen sat with two of our close friends a few feet behind us. They had wanted to be there for moral support.

After the mediator had explained the proceedings, detailing the case and the settlement, we were given time to privately discuss if and how we wanted to continue. My sons and I stood in the separate room and I quietly studied their faces as I thought about the weight of my decision. This was my call. The entire case was up to me.

God, what do I do? You have to tell me what to do. What's best for my family? This is so much bigger than me and I don't know what to do.

Dusty looked exhausted and worn-out. Josh seemed as though there was still some fight left in him, but he was tired too. They both had been through so much and I didn't want them to keep dealing with any more of this legal mess.

"What do you want to do?" I asked them softly.

They looked at each other and then back at me. "I'm done. I can't do it anymore," Dusty said emphatically.

"I can't either," I agreed. "Josh, are you okay with this?"

"Yah, I'm done," Josh replied quietly.

"Okay. We're done." I said with finality and we walked back into the mediation room together. I looked at each of the men sitting in front of me and felt my stomach flutter nervously from what I was about to say. I took a deep breath to steady myself and began my story.

I gave them the account of what the last three-and-a-half years had felt like for my family and me. I described the hole Ben's death had left in all of our lives. I wanted them to know what they had taken from me, my boys, my granddaughter, and Ben's parents, and that Ben was not just an occupational hazard they had to conceal or clean up. He was a human being that had lived a precious and fulfilling life.

I didn't want to shame them, claim my vengeance or throw my own pity party. Although, I could have easily made the meeting about me if I hadn't worked through forgiving the flight nurse and company beforehand. I had to let them go and surrender my rights once again; otherwise the wounds leftover from their incompetence would fester inside me and I wouldn't heal.

What if my son Josh is in that predicament? He was an EMT, a first responder, and mistakes happen. He or any of his crewmembers could be responsible for a preventable death some day.

Just a few weeks before Ben's accident, I had my own encounter of nearly hitting a pedestrian with my car. In the blink of an eye, I could've killed that person and been charged with vehicular homicide as well.

Forgiving the flight team wouldn't have been possible, unless I had forgiven God first. I had *accepted his acceptance* and forgiveness for hating him, and in turn, I was free to forgive myself and others. The debts I could've held against the company were to suffer as I had suffered. I wanted to put them out of business by suing them for every penny they were worth. Even the one thing I felt they owed me, they could not give me. *They couldn't bring Ben back to life.*

As I spoke, I heard sniffles from my family beside and behind me. I knew my sons had never heard me talk about the details of my grief, the depth of my pain and loss, and the impact it was having on me.

I was sad while I addressed them because I was still in mourning, but the fact that I could stand here and express genuine mercy to the people responsible for killing Ben, was both a humbling and honoring experience. I was given the opportunity to validate Ben's existence, and hopefully prevent another wrongful death to a family like ours by telling my story.

When I was ready to conclude, I looked directly into the air flight company owner's eyes that were now brimming with tears. "You may not need to hear this, but I need to say it. For whatever part you played in Ben's death, I forgive you and I release you," I said boldly. "You don't owe me anything further. It's done."

After the mediation was officially adjourned, the owner approached me and asked if he could shake my hand. I consented and instead of a cordial handshake, he gave me a politely distanced hug. Then he and his lawyers gathered their belongings and exited the room.

I signed more legal documents than I could count, and then we were free to leave. I felt relieved that this huge chapter of my life had ended, but I was sad too. The end of our lawsuit was another finality to Ben's death, and nothing in my circumstances had changed. But even though Ben was still gone and I felt the same, or so I thought, I couldn't deny the redemption happening within me.

Through the weeks and months that followed, my healing continued flourishing and was apparently starting to overflow from the inside out. People were beginning to take notice.

Friends and family members started dropping hints about men they knew, and suddenly everyone had an uncle, brother, boss, cousin, neighbor, or co-worker I needed to meet. The not-so-subtle suggestions to get out and date were beginning to wear on me.

Three years ago, I had agreed to go on a blind date. I gave in to the expectation that I should be ready for dating, but I didn't know how to date after being married for thirty-one years. I had cried for three days leading up to the date because it was something I *had* to do, and not something I *wanted* to do. I wasn't nervous, probably because I drank a few shots before he had arrived, but I wasn't excited either.

The man was nice enough and very understanding when I told him we wouldn't be seeing each other again. I had spent the next three days in a sobbing mess with the realization that I was not at all ready to date. I was still too married. Ben was still too present. For a while, I was scared something was wrong with me because I wasn't ready. I had another widow friend who was happy and vibrant because she was putting herself out there.

> Would I be like her if I dated around? Could I feel happy again if I landed a man?

But I didn't want to throw myself in a relationship just to feel better; that felt extremely selfish and needy. A loving, thriving relationship wasn't about attaching my needs to someone else and sucking the life out of them just to get those needs met. I didn't operate that way.

True healing was the only road. The passing of time, comparing myself to other widows, or the expectations of other's and my own could not determine my readiness.

I decided to surrender my questioning concerning the next man in my life over to God. I didn't know what I was doing anyway and would probably get in his way or screw something up.

Instead of asking God who, what, when, where, and how did he want to bring someone into my life? I switched to asking what he was doing in me. Soon after, my fear of dating changed into fear of falling in love again.

> What if I fell in love, married, and then he died? What if

I was widowed again? *Was love worth the risk?*

But I was ready. I had days when I lost myself in fantasizing the perfect scenario where I would meet someone; we would go out, laugh, relax, and just enjoy each other's company. Then I knew I was trying to escape the loneliness. I had been on several other dates. I had a good time, the guys were perfectly pleasant, but not my type. I was ready to be with a man, to have someone to play tennis with, go play an evening round of golf, a boat ride on the lake at sunset, someone to spend the weekends with, or go on last-minute vacations.

Some days I let the frustration get to me, especially on weekends because they had always been restful, relaxing, partying and fun. That was when I felt most alone. God had promised me he would meet my needs, but they sure didn't feel met at times.

> He told me I trusted him enough to hate him, but what about trusting him enough to love again? And how long did he want me to wait?

Patience was not my forte or virtue. Waiting on God felt extremely ominous. He didn't function in the lines and spaces of my calendar. I had patience only because I knew I had to be, but I didn't have peace in the unknown.

> Was I supposed to be doing something while I waited, dating around like everyone was telling me to? Or was I supposed to sit and be still while God did his thing?

Now, the days were becoming consistently better. I had surrendered my relationship status, even though my family members hadn't, and allowed myself and God to take care of me. I could trust God with his timing and let go of my constant questioning. "Wait" was still my personal four-letter-word, but I felt peaceful more often than not. Anger was no longer my go-to emotion.

I was learning how to pamper myself. I used to say yes to everyone and everything out of duty and expectation, but lately I could actually do what I wanted to do. I was more in tune with my emotions. I learned how to say no and take time for me. Whether it was getting a massage, having my nails done, not answering the phone when it rang, or saying I don't have time for lunch this week. I could put my ear buds in with my favorite music, go outside and, without feeling guilty, I didn't let anyone who walked slower than me to come along.

When I counseled, I was able to identify with those who had suffered a loss of someone they loved dearly, a child, or a spouse. I could look them in the eyes and feel the connection, *the fellowship of suffering*, without having to shut down my emotions, run away, or feel uncomfortable. I looked forward to sitting with someone through the painful silence of their grief. I enjoyed the focus shifting onto someone else's pain besides mine.

Hope was starting to come alive in me. I had known what hope was not since Ben's death; through desperation and wanting to end my life, doubting God, and hating my own misconception of him. Now I was discovering a deeper hope; through surrender and desiring a new life, trusting God, and allowing him to redefine himself in me.

I began realizing that I had control over **nothing,** and was truly living a surrendered life. I was free in every sense of the word. I had finally given my grieving, anger, and expectations over to God.

Dwelling in that space of total surrender was incredible for me. I didn't obsess or worry about fixing myself anymore, or even trying to, because I knew he would do it.

I was no longer afraid or frustrated about my future, hiding in my past, or just existing by the clock. I was living each day as they came and I could be present again.

The journey of discovering hope and surrender between God and I had been through my grieving. I was at the point where I didn't hold anything back from him. Whether it was love or hate, passion or indifference, surrender or anger, hope or grief, joy or pain; he could handle it all. I had learned that although God was inherently good, he was not necessarily safe.

I never thought I would live to say I survived widowhood. I was still a widow, but it didn't define my anymore.

God was pursuing me, as he had all along, and now I wasn't resisting him. I was beginning to let him be my Ishi like he had promised. No matter how many times I had cursed him and hated his being, he never left me. He showed me how he hurt with me. He felt what I felt.

Somehow we became more intimate through my pain.

He was closer to me and more real than my faulty conception of him before Ben's death. We knew each other better, and our relationship deepened through tragedy and brokenness.

Completely emptied and left for dead, I had gone through the fire and God went in with me. I emerged on the other side with a few scars, but I had been restored in him.

I was alive and experiencing real life like I had never thought possible.

After Life

The spiritual meaning of every situation is not what happens to us, but what we do with what happens to us and who we decide to become because of what happens to us.
~ Marianne Williamson

Today, six years after Ben's death, I can tell you I am not who I was.

Before experiencing the ruthless pain of death and betrayal, I lived independent with God, co-existing instead of allowing him to be in an intimate relationship with me. My journey through grief was *more* than I could humanly handle; unlike the popular verse that says God *won't* give me more than I can bear...

I'm glad he did.

If that passage were true, then I would've never been broken. I wouldn't have learned to let go of everything I thought I controlled, and have complete dependence on him.

Last year I had a White Funeral to say good-bye to the "woman that was" at Ben's gravesite with the ladie's group from Simply Grace. I realized the lie that I had buried the best parts of me with my husband, I needed to mourn the *old* Bekki (that some still want me to be) in order to celebrate the new woman blossoming from the ashes of my shame.

I carry two regrets in my life after Ben. The first is I wish I would've cremated Ben's remains and spread his ashes over the Badlands in

South Dakota, instead of burying him in a gravesite. Ben had taken a road trip on his motorcycle out to the Badlands and fell in love with the area.

The second regret is I could not be what my sons, Josh and Dusty, needed me to be through these six years. In a way I had felt selfish believing I needed to make myself priority number one. But I quickly learned that misbelief was religion trying to put false guilt on me.

I couldn't put my grieving pains aside for the sake of others. I wasn't going to be a martyr. I learned that I had to heal before I could be there for my family. Today, they are finding healing in their own ways and I am blessed to have a part in their journey.

The process of telling my story has been challenging to say the least. The same fears of being exposed and vulnerable to others still haunt me now, but at the same time, I am being freed. Knowing people will read and see what my hate and grieving looked like is terrifyingly exciting.

I have learned that grief and forgiveness are not one-time events. They aren't as clean or calculable as I would like them to be, but messy mosaics of difficult truths and honest feelings.

I still have hard times when all I want to do is isolate from my life, family, and the world. However, I don't camp out there like I did in the past. Now I can choose. Now I have peace.

God helped me discover a strength inside of me that I never knew existed. I am not afraid of being alone anymore...

and God and I slow dance together.

My desire for anyone who happens upon this book is that you will realize the freedom within you to be real with yourself, God, and others, and the courage to be transparent with the emotions, thoughts, and beliefs you carry.

My hope is for you to discover the meaning of true acceptance, grace, and love, and that you would remain open to receive these mysterious gifts, because they appear in the unlikeliest of people and places.

My prayer is that you will find a community that allows you to question and search, and embraces and loves you exactly where you're at in life.

If you have any questions, comments, insights, or want to share your story, we would appreciate your feedback. Please send us an e-mail to:
contact@thegodhaterbook.com